Gordon Lightfoot Biography: Harmony in the Spotlight

"Every time you wanted to do something, you'd hope it would score. You'd keep trying and trying, and all of the sudden, something would come right out of left field, like 'The Wreck of the Edmund Fitzgerald.' No one had any idea about that one."

- *GORDON LIGHTFOOT -*

By **HEATHER MARIE PETERSEN**

D1706203

CONTENTS

PROLOGUE

THE END OF THE WEEKEND

PROLOGUE

September 20, 2011/Review October 19, 2011 — Dave Bidini, an accomplished writer and a founding member of the Canadian band, the Rheostatics, has written a unique book, which is part musical history, and part Gordon Lightfoot biography.

It is the story of the 1972 Mariposa Festival, a review of news events during one week in July 1972 that culminated in the festival, and a biography of Gordon Lightfoot written without any contact with him, which is rare for a living subject. Regardless of how unlikely it may seem that this is a recipe for success, Bidini manages to carry it off. To make it work, his "bio" of Lightfoot is in the form of "letters" he, Bidini, may have written to Lightfoot.

Bidini is a very entertaining author who is simultaneously pensive, perceptive, and engaging. While the events (historical and biographical) are drawn from reputable sources, many are imprecise, and Bidini fills in the gaps with imagined details, weaving a plausible story while letting the reader know which details are factual and which are the product of his fertile imagination.

MONDAY JULY 10TH

They walked outside at 3:21 p.m. on Monday, brandishing tinfoil periscopes, kleenex dispensers, and hole-polka-dotted cigar boxes. A child stood on a hill, holding an empty bandage box with a slivered opening at one end, its contents spilling at his ankles, waiting for the universe to consume itself. Others eschewed such crude devices, glued and taped at kitchen tables and workbenches, preferring to simply tent their fingers above their brows as they stared bravely, foolishly, at the sun, which would vanish completely a few hours past North American midday in the slow molasses of a moment. The illuminated globe would darken except for a strip of gold that danced around the edges of the moon - the new moon - before the eclipse held in the sky like a celestial motorist stopped to gaze down at everyone else looking up. Their eyes were counting the seconds. The entire globe has been compressed into a single immobile black shape.

Darkness fell in other areas of the world, too, including Orissa, in Northeastern India, where Kabari merchant Abdi Sultan lay on a bamboo mat in his wooden home on Monday, waiting for the eclipse to cool the scorching grounds of his little Gadjat hamlet. His ancestors had built Abdi's hamlet out of the Chandaka jungle, which was home to chitals, barking deer, wild pigs, rhesus monkeys, rudder mongoose, crested serpent eagles, pangolins, Indian wolves, rock pythons, Bengal lizards, and the world's largest elephant reserve. The year 1972 had provided a painfully hot summer, and drought had deprived villagers and surrounding wildlife of their most basic requirements, which is why Abdi was hopeful that the day's celestial event would help to ease the season's torpor. As time passed, he noticed the shadows above him growing longer and the edges of the sky becoming darker as the moon approached its white-hot target. Abdi closed his eyes, placed a sabatari leaf on his tongue, and crossed his arms over his chest. Top and bottom, up and down, north and south, and past and future all blended together, and anything that wasn't deeply entrenched in the dirt darkened as if dipped in a pot of black ink. If the darkness comforted Abdi, it terrified the forest's beasts, notably the elephants, who had likewise suffered from the heat and dryness and for whom the eclipse provided no relief. Instead, the abrupt darkness in the sky was like the final act of a tremendous and scary power. Abdi heard the gigantic monsters' footfalls and thought nothing of it at first. But the sound became louder, and the elephants' footfalls became more rushed and stressed: the elephants were going insane. The light of day ultimately returned, but twenty-four villagers had been trampled to death by the time Monday turned into Tuesday. The Chandaka villages were destroyed.

The men were released in the late afternoon to play softball; something about inmates' rights, as well as recreation and exercise. When it was first erected, the field was a source of debate in the town because it was superior to many of the county's diamonds, complete with lighting, groomed base paths, and a new, pristine dish for home plate. The inmates dubbed their squad the Sabres, or so the warden allowed. The Portsmouth House Petes, a team sponsored by a local hotel, provided the day's competition, though others questioned why anyone would voluntarily venture beyond the barbed wire fences into the area. And, while prison officials thought softball was a peaceful sport, the inmates were not convinced. A bat wasn't a toy to them, not when it was handled by someone like Donald Oag, who'd killed two inmates during the Kingston Pen riots of '71, and whose face had been bludgeoned flat by despair and rage after a lifetime spent among shitty people and horrible parents. Holding the bat reminded him, and others like him, of throwing a large wooden plank against a small amphibian too sluggish and dim-witted to move; or how the tire iron sounded as it landed on the thug's back, whom he beat harder, then hit some more. Oag despised his life and attempted suicide multiple times while in prison. He was a cruel and tortured guy, not without issues.

The psychiatrists and doctors employed by Millhaven explained to the warden that playing baseball was about tension release, or transference of rage, or some other nonsense, because, really, you'd have to be the dumbest rube alive to believe that any of that would work on these hard cases. If the game accomplished anything, it was that the inmates and guards might, if only for a few seconds, forget the misery of their situation, because only a few feet of metal fence separated those who slept behind bars at night and those who, at the end of the day, were able to go home in freedom to their wives and families, which some suggested was no freedom at all.

In 1972 America, freedom was a go-to word. It had a silver belt buckle, a red, white, and blue bumper sticker, and endless slogans advertising innumerable products: Ride the Free Skies, The Freedom Trail, The Taste of Freedom, and Freedom's Just Another Word for Kris Kristofferson and Janis Joplin's Music. People lived in the world of Dick Allen and Evel Knievel, Woodward and Bernstein, where they could be themselves. Freedom meant huge cars for everyone, fast food that didn't kill you (yet), gleaming new liquor stores selling beer and spirits in mixed-race neighborhoods, The Happy Hooker, Grand Funk Railroad, key parties, cigarettes that made you tall, handsome, and popular (and didn't kill you; yet), and slow-mo color-drenched NFL films broadcast on TV stations that began with either w or k. While most Americans spent the early hours of July 10 staring at the sky looking for the eclipse, a few dozen stared deeper at a tiny spacecraft scuttling farther into the galaxy than anything that had come before it.

NASA named it Pioneer 10, albeit the designation was based as much on wishful thinking as anything else. The spacecraft's mission was to fly beyond Mars and into Jupiter's asteroid belt, becoming the first artificial object to depart the solar system. The odds were unimpressive. Pioneer 10 was launched from Complex 36A Cape Canaveral on March 2, 1972, and crossed Mars' orbit sometime in June. On July 10, MIT and UCLA bioengineers, mathematicians, physicists, and aeronautic architects sat staring at a Dr. Strangelove tracking screen, smoking cigarettes and drinking sweetened coffee from styrofoam cups, waiting to see if the spacecraft would maintain its trajectory and move through the asteroid belt, avoiding rocks as small as an office chair and as large as Alaska, moving at fearsome speeds, something that no spacecraft had done before. They waited a little longer after a few days passed. More coffee, please.

On Monday, Mariposa Folk Festival officials sat in their offices, staring over a map of the weekend's lineup: who would play where, when, and with whom. Mariposa was named after the fictional town in Stephen Leacock's lasting classic, Sunshine Sketches of a Little Town, and was first conceived in 1961 in Orillia, a village on the shores of Lake Simcoe. Every year since its inception had been unique, but the 1971 event was unique in a new way. The festival lost $4,000 that weekend due to confrontations generated by sixties hold-over supporters who thought the festival was becoming too large and protested increasing ticket costs and an emphasis on famous performances to carry the weight. The organizers measured the acts on paper while staring at the performance grid, and everything appeared fine to them. Traditional blues - Roosevelt Sykes and Bukka White - were plentiful, as were banjo workshops, Newfie songs and stories, the legendary country combo Hazel and Alice, and the Mississippi Fife and Drum group. Along with McLauchlan and Cockburn, Bonnie Raitt, who was discovered by Kris Kristofferson and managed by Paul Anka, was scheduled to perform for the first time in Canada. Drawing a box around these performances, the men and women sat for the first time without their artistic director, den mother, and guiding light, Estelle Klein, and rested their pens on the table, confident that the festival would go off without hiccups. There would be no celebrities or surprises. They awaited Friday.

Roger Begin was looking forward to Friday. He was longing for Tuesday. No, he was looking forward to tomorrow. Long-haired and free-spirited – probably rainbow-bandana, too – Roger spent his Monday evening lying torched on the cool sheets of a hospital bed in Ottawa. The day before, Sunday, had been the worst of his life. It had begun well, even exhilaratingly. As he jumped for the first time under the supervision of the Sports Ontario Skydiving School, the nineteen-year-old quivered with fear, tried not to vomit, and imagined himself standing at God's shoulder while waiting at the lip of the plane's door, which a man in goggles had thrown open for him. Roger looked for his parents in the fields below, but they were lost in the land's gigantic and gorgeous quilt work, which lay 2,500 feet below. After the goggled man counted to ten, Roger sprang heroically, inexcusably, and possibly foolishly.

Jennifer Mitchell, eighteen, let herself get swallowed up by her bean bag chair as she spun the record in her palms, giant clam-sized headphones hooked to her sandy-blonde hair. She hadn't heard Dylan in a long time, and his music seemed antiquated for the first time, despite the fact that he was still indisputably the best poet of his generation. The vinyl had also been worn out, with the needle with the penny taped to it dragging itself across side one, then side two, which she celebrated by smoking a roach she'd discovered poking out from the edge of a Persian rug given to her by an old boyfriend who'd brought it home from a trip to Marrakesh. Jenn wondered if she was growing nostalgic at eighteen, a thought that terrified and appalled her, edging too close, she worried, to becoming one of the Old Persons, under whose rules she suffered every day. She tossed the Highway 61 tone arm. Revisited into her vinyl pile with as little movement as possible, then pancaked Led Zeppelin onto the turntable's rubber surface. Electric guitars, indeed. "Dazed and Confused" made her question why she'd decided to go to Mariposa in the first place, but Terry and Janice would be there. It was, at the very least, a weekend away from the Old People, which couldn't be all bad.

Meanwhile, Roger had passed out. The plane sailed out across the robin's egg blue sky, the wind screaming. He'd been told to be exact with the parachute settings, and because he was so close to the ground, he could clearly see his target, which lay like a large red eye on the matted grass of Perth Municipal Airport. But Roger's demise captured his attention. It was the journey of journeys, an emptying of all consciousness and rationality, a denial of weight and matter. Roger closed his eyes. He wondered if this was how he felt the second time through the birth canal.

Roger deviated. He carried on drifting. He opened his eyes and looked for the target, but it was not here. He was seized by the wind and hurled forward, backward, up and down. As he fell, the target became smaller, and he focused his attention between his legs, where tangled hydro cables awaited like a large electric net. His parents yelled into the air, pointing below. Roger continued to plummet, fall, fall, until his body was impaled on the hot trunk wires and 44,000 volts of electricity surged through his bones. Rescuers eventually located him and dragged his body to the ground. They were doing so when they heard a deep shunk that shivered the hydro pole. On Jennifer's turntable, Bonzo's drums slurved to a standstill two kilometers away. The lights went out in the Old People's Home, causing a different kind of eclipse. Before falling back asleep, the young girl stirred slightly. She had plenty of time before she had to leave for Toronto.

On Monday, a teenager named Doug McClement pushed his long hair back on his shoulders, righted the glasses he'd worn since he was a kid, and wrote in his diary: "Back to school. Got 40% on an economics exam. Worked 6 – 10 p.m." A few days later, he "took Glenna MacKenzie to see Jesse Winchester at the Razor's Edge." The next day, he "bought a Sony 336 tape deck," trading in his Wharfedale W30D speaker.

When Doug wasn't being anything other than a typical sixteen-year-old kid living in Kingston, he was schlepping his bass amp into the ass-end of whatever crappy van Country Comfort used to travel from gig to gig. Despite all that was happening in his city and his country and the world, Doug's concerns were mostly musical. He was already starting to feel a little left behind, because, he remembered: "The times were changing enormously in 1972. Rock and roll was growing up, maturing. After a while, we were playing 170 nights a year, which was a lot considering that I was going to university at the time. When I'd first started playing around Ontario in the late sixties, it was very different. You'd do three forty-minute sets, and then two twenty-minute sets. You got the attention of agents and managers by going to their offices and playing for them. My band did this once, for the agent Billy O'Connor, at a place on Gerrard Street, near Maple Leaf Gardens. Seventy-one was actually the beginning of it, when the drinking age went down from twenty-one to eighteen. Bars were switching from country and folk acts to rock acts, and, on the first night of the lowered drinking age, I remember going into the Frontenac Hotel and a waiter asking me, 'So what do you want?' I remember telling him, 'Umm, I don't really know.' Our gigs changed. Before the new clubs opened up, we acted as a back-up band for strippers in places like The Village Pump in Shannonville. At the New Byrne Hotel, which was in Arnprior, the girls would put money in the jukebox and dance to their favorite songs and, sometimes, if the song ended, they had to reach over and put in more money. We played with one stripper whose nickname was 'The Tempest' and she would come out of a coffin. We also backed up a six-foot-four black woman who used the handle 'Rikki Covette, the World's Tallest Stripper.' There was a band called Mainline, which featured Mike McKenna and Mendelson Joe, and they used to play a burlesque show called the Bump N Grind Revue at a place called the Victory. That ended in '72. It was the last vestige of that scene and that vibe, of the old Toronto Telecaster blues sound. Everything was different after 1972. I remember seeing Hall and Oates and noticing that they had road cases, whereas before, bands carried their stuff in old circuses, or railway trunks. Seventy-two was the end of the sixties DIY mentality. Bands now had sound technicians and monitors; semi-pro lighting rather than using Christmas spotlights stolen off their neighbors' front yards. The Stones tour was the first hugely grossing rock and roll tour. And we all know how that monstrosity turned out."

On Monday, the beast rested. things had started badly in vancouver, when the band was denied permission to land in british columbia. officials cited errors in the flight manifest, so they called in trudeau to help, but he was fuckin' useless. the band was forced to land in washington state, run the gauntlet of customs, and when they arrived at pacific coliseum, the vagabonds were attacking the cops, two thousand non-ticket holders savaging the entrance to the arena by hurling bottles, rocks and, according to philip norman, huge lumps of iron. the city said no more of them ever, and no led zeppelin either, which meant that robert plant would never see nat bailey stadium, as if he gave a fuck in the first place. from there, the biggest tour of all time moved on, dragging countless fans and whores and dope dealers and doctors and chefs and soul vampires and robert frank and truman capote, all of them like filthy tassels on the fringe of a old weathered robe hung with rhinestones and coke spoons. big was its mantra; big was its engine. summer crowds from knoxville to fort worth to chicago watched suntanned and barefoot and stoned and horny, or so they looked flashing on tv screens across north america when we watched the news after supper: gawd don't let them go towards that, thought mom and dad, biting their nails. There were drug busts and fights and it was all dirty, really dirty. The kids were camel-toed and devil-horned, juiced by radio ads with the sound of jet plane engines going nnrrgggrrrrrr to the throaty growl of the former bandstand announcer who would die horribly of esophageal cancer a few years later. The sign through the windshield dust said Cincinnati this way as the buses shot north, trundling and nodding at high speeds. The beast was bloated, fat, but you could see its ribs and its cock if you looked closely. That summer, everyone looked closely. it was the stones. It was '72. They slouched into ohio.

Al Mair was less busy on Monday than he was on most days. Gordon Lightfoot, his famous client, hadn't been touring much, having withdrawn from performances following his bout with Bell's palsy. But Mair was fine with the break. Most of his life had already been captivated by rock and roll, humping records when the industry was still in its infancy. "When I first started," he explained, "I would call a radio station and play a song over the phone." I'd mail it to them if they committed to add it to their playlist. If they got it but didn't put it in, I was supposed to ask them to return it. Because a single manufacturing cost was just ten or fifteen cents, the long-distance call would have been more expensive than simply writing it off. When 'Love Me Do' originally came out, we sold 121 copies. It was a little tense until the re-release. The only time it was broadcast was on CFRB 'Calling All Britons.'

"I worked for a week at London Records. Their Ontario distributor, Max Zimmerman, had got into the record business when he ran a variety store on Queen Street, selling vinyl. Back then, I owned a red convertible that had a record player under the dash. The tone arm was heavy so that the record wouldn't skip when I drove, but it destroyed the vinyl. Still, the music sounded great coming out of those speakers. I'd park outside at the drive-in restaurant at Six Points Plaza in Etobicoke and play records like 'Since I Met You Baby' by Ivory Joe Hunter, 'Don't Worry Baby' by the Beach Boys, 'Let's Go, Let's Go, Let's Go' by Hank Ballard and the Midnighters, and an obscure instrumental called 'Straight Flush' by the Frantics. Local bands would play at places like the Concord Tavern. The Concord was where Ronnie Hawkins did his shows, and Saturday afternoons were all the rage. There was a dance floor in the middle, and, on one side, kids could get soda pop and chips for fifty cents, and on the other side, you could drink, although the line often blurred. You'd bring in a mickey and everyone would have a great time. Ronnie would bring up all of these great Southern rock and roll guys – guys like Ersel Hickey and Bobby Schwab (a.k.a. Bobby Starr) – and moonwalk across the stage wearing a beautiful suit. It was the beginning of what is now the Toronto rock and roll scene, where you have thousands of bands playing, everything happening seven nights a week. But back then, there was the Hawk and a few others. But that was it. It was all very new. I can't say that, by the seventies, it was old. But it had definitely changed. The business, the music, everything."

On Monday, Lightfoot slept, most likely in his apartment in the roundhouse building behind the Gardens, or perhaps in the apartment across the street, which had merely a desk and a chair, and some art supplies left behind by his friend, the painter and writer Robert Markle. Lightfoot endured a difficult year in 1972. First, there was the Grammys catastrophe of 1971, which he still felt the aftereffects of. Organizers had asked him to perform his slow, aching hit ballad, "If You Could Read My Mind," on their global awards broadcast, but there was a catch: the show runners wanted to know if he'd consider cutting it to under two minutes, giving advertisers the time they needed to sell stuff to a generation that loved stuff more than any other. Canada's most famous and important songwriter - at least, that's what he'd been before Harvest, Blue, and Music From Big Pink, although he'd always be the first, no matter what anyone else did - paused for a moment (probably even less) to decide that if he was going to take shit from anyone, it wouldn't be the American Academy of the Recording Arts, or whatever ill-gotten group dictated its nation's musical tastes. His refusal meant he'd be kicked from the show, denying himself an international television audience. No one knows how much anxiety this caused him, but his former manager, Al Mair, claims it didn't register within his organization. "To be honest, I don't recall much of a fuss, at least not internally." Gordon, on the other hand, did anything he wanted. He made the judgments and desired complete control over his career."

Something else happened a few months later that may or may not have been caused by the previous eveae first set. The doctor diagnosed him with Bell's palsy, a facial nerve paralysis that affects one's capacity to regulate muscles in the face. Trauma and emotional disorders are typical causes of Bell's palsy, and while Lightfoot could rage and get wild like the best of them, he was also a bottled-up soul.

By the end of the game (the Petes defeated the Sabres, 10-2), fourteen men had fled, making it the greatest jail break in Ontario history. The guard who discovered the little gaps in the fence thought the convicts had vanished into thin air, but the escape was more planned. And it's not like anyone saw it coming. Charles Boomer, who was serving a 37-year prison sentence for armed robbery, used to wander around telling anyone who would listen, "Fellas, I'm going on holiday."

The males had strayed into a corner during the softball game, blind to at least one of the moving tower floodlights. They'd snuck across the fence while the audience applauded their fellow inmates' folly. The soldiers rolled past three spools of barbed wire at the bottom of the fence - how they missed being eviscerated is still unknown - and ran into the bush a few hundred feet distant. Streto Dzambas was one of the escapees. He was twenty-five years old but appeared ten years older, serving a life sentence for murdering a Yonge Street dishwasher, Trevor Poll, with a crowbar and leaving him to die on the wet kitchen floor before reaching into Poll's trousers for the fifty dollars he kept on hand in case he wanted a seat at the Spadina Chinese card game. Dzambas felt another convict, Ronald Fillion, close behind him as he ran towards the prison's surrounding fields and the neighborhoods beyond. Both men were on the verge of hyperventilating, their heated lungs beating against their necks, and it wasn't until they were a safe distance from the prison walls that they spotted a low fog descending, a view that brought them solace in the midst of their terror. Dzambas ran, and Ronald followed, defying the group's plan to scatter. But the assassin had already planned for such an act, knowing that while Ronald was young and crazy enough to cut the wires, even if it meant spending a lifetime in prison, he was also too weak and afraid to ever be alone once he was outdoors. "Streets, we did it!" Ron said, breaking another rule: keep as quiet as possible when running. This was too much for Dzambas. He clenched his fists at his sides and swung, a crack breaking the silence of the night. Ronald sank to the ground, clutching his face as the sound of Dzambas' footsteps faded with each stride. The youngster rose up, pressing the flat of his hand against his cheek, and tried to establish his equilibrium despite the fact that the world was bent sideways.

On Monday, John Singleton did something he'd wanted to do since he was arrested and imprisoned three years ago. There hadn't been a significant escape from Collins Bay - fifteen miles west of Millhaven - in years, so he believed the facility was weak, and that if he tried, he might be able to surprise the guards. He rushed from the jail grounds, cutting through the fence, before slowing to a walk along the CN rail line near Ernestown Station, turning east towards Kingston rather than west towards Belleville. The fugitive walked and walked, or rather floated, across the tall grass beside the dark forest stand, barefoot. He walked and wandered some more until he saw a tracking dog, which charged at his heels. Then a swarm of OPP police appeared, shouting and drawing their weapons. They were involved in the largest manhunt in Canadian jail history, albeit one for someone other than him.

In Monday's late edition, the Globe and Mail reported that "one of the big losers in the 14-man breakout was the prison's softball team, which lost its top pitcher, Richard 'Buddy' Smith, thirty-two, of Petrolia. Smith had appeared in all sixteen Circle Softball League games for the prison team before joining the others who escaped from prison. The escape came after Smith suffered his worst defeat of the season. The loss cost the Sabres sole possession of first place in the seven-team league. Murray Black, who smashed a home run and two singles off Smith, said after the game: 'I wouldn't say that he (Smith) was jittery, however, I don't think he was himself. He didn't move the ball around at all, just throwing straight strikes. I was talking to him after and I told him that I'd see him Thursday (for the next game). But Smith didn't answer. He just grinned. Now I know why.' "

LETTER IN WHICH I ASK YOU ABOUT PLAYING MASSEY HALL STUFF

Hello, Gord. This is the first paragraph of the letter. I'm not going to start where most biographies start because, I dunno, all those books that go on to describe the legend playing with his toys and burning his hand on the stovetop and how his Grade Three teacher threw a ruler at him and the time he wet his pants coming home from school and what his dog's name was and how he saw his uncle die in a horrible chipper accident and what he did when he got his first report card; I dunno. I always want the writer to get to the bottom of why somebody would want to write a book about that individual in the first place. In your case, it's the music and the songs. Playing the guitar. Words. Concerts. Canada, radio. Mariposa. Drugs, love, and alcohol. And other things.

So I imagine you as a pre-teen kid, sitting on the quilt at the edge of your bed, dressed in ill-fitting brown cords your mom bought for you at the Buy Right, playing a guitar that came out of a long cardboard box, trying to find great sweeping chords to match the fullness of the infinite sky, even though the sound you made was more like sprrrngggtt! because your hands hurt and the tips of your fingers were sore, but screw it: your grandparents and their grandparents and their grandparents before them had dug their mitts deep into the hard rich soil to build a life for their sons and daughters, and because they did, you sat there and played: an A chord struck with the E string unexpectedly opened, releasing a long broad note at the foot of the neck, reminding you of a tern swallowed by the water's horizon as your mother tapped on the door and said, "Phone call, son. It's Whelan," (I know your friend's name was Whelan because it was stated in that other book about you, If You Could Read His Mind, by Maynard Collins, which was released twenty years ago). You talked to Whelan, then went back to your room, propped your guitar against the cowboy-wallpapered wall, put on your boots, and walked over to your friend's house ("Bye, Mom"), where you played board games with him at the kitchen table. Whelan claimed he loved the new song by Buddy

Knox, the small guy with the beard, but you weren't sure. There are no gulls. There are no lakes. There will be no stillness. I believe you were twelve years old. Life was progressing, though you'd be damned if you knew where.

You enjoyed singing and running. I did as well. Don't all 12-year-olds? Glenn Gould, perhaps, but still. You went to St. Paul's United Church in Orillia for junior choir rehearsal. I imagine the old pastor in dark robes taking you aside and telling you that you sang like an angel, and just hearing the word - angel - gave you a strange feeling: a soft word coming from such a severe man, a word he'd let pass through his lips and over his teeth because your voice had somehow found a place between his rib cage and heart, and maybe it was then that you understood how music worked and why it had lasted forever, despite the changing world and I read somewhere that you sang high - way high - filling neighborhood churches as the congregation swooned to the sound of your voice twirling around the molding at the top of the church columns the way Aretha Franklin's, Little Richard's, or Sam Cooke's did, even though you didn't know their names yet. Besides, their voices had been boiled in the filthy heat of the American South, whereas yours had been born in the freezing cold, something you didn't know either, not yet, and maybe you're discovering it for the first time now, but maybe not, because I have no idea if you're reading this. During church service, you could see your mother and father sitting in the pews, Mom looking proud and Dad, well, Dad just being Dad, as all fathers are, as you raised your chin with your hands hanging like scarves at your sides and felt your diaphragm fill then empty then fill again the way your uncle worked the bellow raising fire from the hearth. During Parents' Day at West Ward public school, they played a recording of you singing "An Irish Lullaby" over the public address system to your friends, classmates, and teachers; pretty much the entire town stood there listening as your soprano rang through the speaker grills at the front of those dry yellow classrooms. If your school was anything like mine - or my kids' - your principal was named King, Jenkins, or Arnold (they were all English back then, the principals), and what you couldn't see was how his demeanor softened as he spared a moment to listen to the tune you'd learned from the prized Weavers record you played three times a day and once at bedtime on your family's four-in-one.

And then you were in Massey Hall a few years later. I also played there. Just saying the name makes me shiver, and I'm curious if it still makes you shiver after all these years of playing it. Wasn't it the first time you sang in a big city? Shuter Avenue. The Allan Gardens. The subway system. Simpson's. Fran's. The Golden Coq. The City Hall. You were only down the street from Maple Leaf Gardens, where Teeder Kennedy used to play and where the woman would ring her bell and cry, "Let's go Teeeeeder!" as he cupped the puck on his stick and charged up the ice. I know this meant a lot to you, Gord, because they made you the celebrity captain of the Toronto Maple Leafs in 1993, and I also know you used to go to games all the time in the 1970s and 1980s because Bill's mom saw you there, just hanging out, no big deal, signing autographs and talking trade. "Hockey games at Maple Leaf Gardens became part of the ritual," wrote Cathy Evelyn Smith (more on her, lots more, later). We'd slog home to the apartment in the snow, hoarse from cheering." I'm not sure whether you know, but I, too, am a Leafs fan. Love. I get flack for it - who doesn't? - especially when I'm on the road doing book tours or playing gigs, but I wonder whether anyone makes fun of you when you're around, being a legend and all. Once, after a show, this guy approached me and gushed about our songs, albums, and concerts, and then before he went, he said, "Shame you're a Leafs fan, though." I believe he was a Habs fan, but I'm not certain. The fucking Habs. Do you despise them as much as I do, Gord? If you're a true Leafs fan - which, according to Bill's mother, you are - you probably despise them as well. Oh, and if you don't want to chat about music or your life, Gord, I'd be happy to sit around and slam the Habs. That way, we could avoid talking about anything actual, even if talking about hockey is more real than most things.

You were back in the car with your parents and older sister, Beverly, after it was finished, and it was late evening, and you thought that maybe something had changed, but maybe not. Your father fiddled with the steering wheel and the radio before looking at you in the rearview mirror and remarking, "Good work tonight, son." Perhaps he didn't tell you anything since he is a guy of few words. That's what they say about your father: he's silent, authoritarian, and as complicated as any guy who ever lived. He used to smack you over the head with a hairbrush. Was it a belt, then? Or even a strap? I've read stories in which each of these is mentioned.

JUESDAY, JULY 11TH

On Tuesday, Anand Chopra, thirty-two, was, according to the Toronto Star, "driving east on Bloor Street when he saw a man standing naked on the wall of the Bloor Viaduct" above the city's Don Valley, a popular spot for jumpers before a protective fence was built in 2003. "People were passing as if nothing was wrong," Mr. Chopra recalled, despite the fact that the man had tossed his garments into the Don River. I decided it didn't matter if someone hit my car, so I came to a halt, raced across to him, and grabbed him by the legs just as he began to jump. Then another man arrived to assist. I was surprised that no one else had come to speak with him." Chopra recalls "the man was in tears." He was overjoyed that we had saved him. He admitted to me that he was despondent. He stated that all he wanted was someone to talk to."

On Tuesday, Team Canada (and ex-Bruins') coach Harry Sinden answered the goddamned phone in his goddamn hotel suite in goddamned Toronto, the heart of the summer, which was supposed to be about burgers and fishing and broads and beers and driving down a gravel road going nowhere, but instead, it was about this goddamned hockey series against the goddamned Russians. Proudfoot from the Star was calling. "This is my team," Harry said, as he had countless goddamned times before. Bobby Hull will be there.

On Tuesday, tall, ponytailed Brent Titcomb drove around France. Brent had traveled there from England via Canada, his scarab beetle totem crammed in the pocket of his pants. He was 32 and had already spent years playing in Yorkville, which he characterized as "a place where you parked your ideas, exchanged thoughts, music, and philosophies with other people your own age." If, by 1972, the idyll had started to rust for others, it hadn't for Brent, who talked about how there were safe houses on every block; psychedelic dropins where, he said, "you'd sit around and get into heavy discussions about life and art, something that I just don't see in today's generation of kids. It was a happy period, and music was evolving. Someone would go down to Sam the Record

Man and get an album, and we'd sit around, get high, and listen to it over and over. Sergeant Pepper's Lonely Hearts Club Band was similar in this regard. You'd hear phrases you'd never heard in a song before, as well as instruments you had no idea existed. Big Pink's music was the same. When I first heard about it, I said to myself, 'They recorded their album in a house?' It had never been done before. There was also Joni and her unusual tunings, as well as the voices in CSNY: such strange harmonic frameworks. Before Dylan and The Band and the Byrds, we'd never heard folk music that had bass and drums before. Those musicians – as well as Ian and Sylvia and Lightfoot – made us realize that we didn't only have to cover songs by other artists; we could write our own. It might seem standard now, but things that are regarded as a given today were actually pretty revolutionary back then. The world was changing in front of our eyes, and I was fortunate to be a part of it."

When Brent awoke the next morning on his way to the airport, he found he only had two contacts in the United Kingdom, one of which was a woman named Carol. "I could have called either number," he explained. "However, I called Carol." When she answered, she said that if I could reach her house in 45 minutes, I could accompany her to meet the Chief Druid, a man named Thomas Maughm. It seemed like a reasonable plan. "Thomas Maughm had a long white beard and eyes that pierced you like electric shocks when he flashed them. He was dressed regularly, but he appeared to be from Lord of the Rings. He exuded a deep, ethereal quality, and others around him were captivated by his presence. I couldn't have realized it at the time, but meeting him was the start of an extraordinary few weeks. Looking back, it was as if seeing him was a warm-up for everything that was going to happen."

Brent met a group of folks after a few days who stated they were headed to Worthy Farm near Glastonbury to attend a new rock festival. Brent joined their caravan after stopping by the home of scholar John Bennett, who had already left for the festival grounds. John was a pupil of George Ivanovich Gurdjieff, a mystic and spiritual teacher whose "Fourth Way" ideology - taken from the Sufi concept of self-awareness - had a large following. Gurdjieff and Bennett both believed that the world had become stunted as a result of individuals losing their ability to see reality, their loss of consciousness being replaced by a form of hypnosis, or, in Gurdjieff's words, "a waking sleep." Brent and his new buddies talked about these ideas as they drove across the English countryside. "Between hearing about John and meeting the Chief Druid, I became immersed in a world of spirituality and mysticism." And when we arrived in Glastonbury, I felt more vibrant, active, and alert than I had in my entire life."

Titcomb put this energy to use at Worthy Farm. "We arrived at the festival early. It wasn't long before I understood that these English kids had no idea how to create shelters for us, especially given what had become of the ground: a vast, muddy soup that made it difficult to walk around. So I went into town, acquired some twine, plastic, and saplings, and erected something that looked like an igloo - or at least a snow lodge - using rocks to hold down the plastic covering. It was essentially what I'd learnt as a child growing up in the forests in West Vancouver, and while everyone was impressed and grateful, it was something I would have done otherwise. The entrance was similar to that of an igloo, however it curled around to keep the wind out. I lit candles to warm the room, and I was really comfortable. The wind was roaring at high speeds outside, and the rain made it appear as if the Earth was about to end.

"The festival organizers wanted to build the stage using the proportions of the Great Pyramid. They situated the stage at the crossroads of two very heavy lay lines, sometimes known as planetary meridians of energy, that ran through the land. They moved it slightly off-center because they were concerned about what kind of energies would be invoked. As the bad weather continued, someone had the bright notion of driving a stake through the precise center of where the lines crossed. The sky cleared almost quickly. It was strange. After that, they needed someone to test the sound system, so they came around to my shelter and asked if I could help. Sure, I said. "I was the first person to ever play live music at what is now regarded as Europe's most famous musical festival," not many people know.

"One of the reasons for going to Europe was to rescue my wife. She'd gotten into trouble and had fallen ill. She'd been working at Bill Wyman's place in Nice, where the Stones were recording Exile on Main Street. After I got her, I knew that I had to get back quickly because of my date at Mariposa, so I ducked to find out when I should return. You see, a dowser asks themselves questions with only yes or no answers, and I was told to fly home on the day of my gig. It seemed crazy – flying from England on the morning of a show in another country – but that's what I did. When I landed in Toronto, I went straight to my set, arriving twenty minutes late. On stage, I told the crowd, 'You might not believe me, but I woke up this morning in Kent, England, and now, folks, here I am.' Of course, everybody probably thought it was just a story, just a line, but it was true. When I finished my set, I walked down the steps from the stage. Standing at the bottom was Joni Mitchell, looking up at me."

If life had been turned upside down at home, things were changing in other places, too, such as Iceland, where on Tuesday, people expected something that hadn't happened in thirty years: an American sitting across from a Russian, fingers tented, heads bowed, trying to read the intimacy of each other's thoughts in an intellectual pas de deux that would become the focus of their respective nations' attention.

Two thousand fans (some of whom had lined up at five a.m. to watch the match) watched as Spassky - sporting a neutral haircut and dressed in a somber suit and vest - moved into his chair to await the arrival of his opponent, who, despite being placated by the increased prize money, was still nowhere to be found. The Russian moved his white pawn nevertheless, then dropped his head and remained motionless until Fischer arrived. The American arrived seven minutes late, sat slumped over the board, snorted, and then made his first move. Hundreds of supporters sat downstairs in the cafeteria, eating breakfast and drinking beer while watching the game on closed-circuit television. They watched even more closely as the American stood up, sought the attention of match officials, and waved a finger at them: the International Chess Federation's blue, white, and red emblem had become a major distraction, not to mention the orange juice, which was lukewarm, and could the organizers please find him some ice cubes? They did (obviously), and the game continued. It burst, with Fischer seizing Spassky's poisoned pawn, leaving his own bishop exposed, and risking a move that would almost certainly result in a clear victory for either side, rather than the draw that both men appeared to be heading for. People argued about Fischer's strategy. Was it clever? Crazy? Manipulative? Wrong-headed? Was Fischer foregoing the game in order to instill false confidence in his opponent, or was he really outmatched? The cafeteria patrons drank their beers and requested more. Those in the corridor sought to calm their racing hearts. Spassky moved his chair and waited for Fischer to answer, but the American stood up and ordered that the television crew working on the stage's side be asked to leave immediately. Why are they being moved now? inquired the organizers. Why not now? Fischer reasoned. Really? C'mon. Jesus. Yes, right now. Really. The organizers declined. Fischer walked out, taking 35 minutes off his time limit. His request was eventually approved (of course it was). When he returned to the chamber, he was obliged to make sixteen moves in twenty-five minutes, all of which were futile. The game was delayed and resumed the next morning, but Fischer had already handed it over to the defending world champion. And so: Capitalists: 0; Russia: 1.

Ray and Bill Newbury, two bachelor farmers, sat in the drawing room of the farmhouse they shared with their 71-year-old mother on Tuesday. The mass escape from the nearby prison changed the way the Newburys saw and heard things: the long grass rustling a little too hard; a bird's cry jangling with alarm; and the soft sweep of the wind growing rough and fingernailed as it crept through old doors and window frames. Homes had been guarded, highways had been closed, and the perimeter of the area had been controlled by a police force attempting not to panic. A photograph on the front page of the July 12th edition of the Toronto Star showed fourteen-year-old Paul Battersby with his dog, Pal, cradling a double-barreled shotgun while sitting on his front porch, ready to defend his sister, twelve-year-old Andrea, should the convicts come to take them hostage (the Battersby parents were on vacation at the time). A group of men lined the edge of the pier on nearby Wolfe Island, a twenty-minute ferry ride from the Kingston mainland, with rifles, but no one could be confident that the fugitives hadn't already crossed.

The Newbury brothers' occupation was dairy farming. It was their entire lives and everything they had ever known. The brothers had forty Holstein cows, which had to be milked whether they were in prison or not. They knew their animals, and they knew them well, so strange sounds - a knocking that happened once, then not again; a depth of lowing that lasted longer than it would have under normal circumstances - made the Newbury brothers turn to each other before they bundled their mother into their car, drove her to a neighbor's house, and returned home to step softly, quietly, through the low grass towards the barn behind the farmhouse, their two shotguns pried open.

Colin Linden arrived home from school on Tuesday and headed directly to the basement. He took out his guitar and began practicing in the suburban home he shared with his mother and brother. Colin practiced constantly, every day. Colin's mother had urged that he go down to Mariposa on the weekend to play the Open Mic stage, despite the fact that he'd never performed in front of anyone before. Colin stated that he would think about it. The spare bedroom in their North York home had been converted into a music room, with only a tiny oak desk for lyric writing, a record player, and Colin's first instrument. In the corner, there was also a couch that rolled out into a bed, which suited Colin as well: a place where, after hours of playing, his young fingers had contorted into strange new shapes on the unforgiving fretboard, he could stretch out and imagine himself as a hardened gig-slave rumbling down the interstate on the back bench of a bus or luxury sedan, instead of twelve years old and seasoned in nothing but sugary cereal, television, and comic books. Even though he hadn't even touched his first tit, he dreamed of being a ragged bluesman.

Tits were everywhere for Bobby Hull, the renowned hockey player. He couldn't stop himself: they were just there. In the 1970s, tits were everywhere: in Klute with Jane Fonda; in Russ Meyer's films; on Paula Prentiss in The Parallax View, which I saw with my parents on vacation in the United States; in R. Crumb's comic books; in the softcore Baby Blue Movies that Citytv showed on Friday nights; in Playboy, Penthouse, Cheri, Oui, and Swank magazines, which the neighborhood smoke-and-gift racked on

Bobby was dubbed the Golden Jet. He'd won the Stanley Cup in 1961 and had become hockey's first playboy throughout the years. When he signed his massive million-dollar novelty check with the new rogue hockey league, the WHA, his Winnipeg team named themselves after him. There were women everywhere. Chicks desired him, and boys wanted to know him. He paid a modest fortune to get gold hair plugs sutured into his head before dressing in suede and velour and signing endorsement arrangements with clothing companies, equipment manufacturers, pizza eateries, and jewelers long before players did. He always gave the autograph boys a wide chuckling smile, the dads a firm handshake, and the ponies and moms a low, sharkish stare. Bobby Hull was the epitome of 1970s hockey. In a game hunting for its telegenic money shot, his slapshot was the widest gesture of panoramic might. He wanted everything and he wanted it immediately, but he was simply acting like any other seventies super-dude. His new league and club would begin in the fall, but first he'd face the Russians. He'd show them Communist scumbags his banana sword. He'd feed them his shot and make them wish they'd never seen such a magnificent Canadian specimen: rich, straight-toothed, farm-raised, and equine-strong. He'd drive Yuri, Sergei, and Igor back to the Turkmen mountains. He'd stay behind with their Svetlanas.

On Tuesday, another famous Canadian playboy - Pierre Elliott Trudeau, who, at fifty-two, was still cool and sideburned, but looked slightly sallow-cheeked and weary-eyed on this day - took a moment to think about nothing. The polls, the newspapers, and the pundits all suggested that Trudeaumania was coming to an end, and to make matters worse, he'd been sent to Prescott, not far from the site of the Millhaven escape, to unofficially launch an election campaign that would result in his governing party losing power, forfeiting a majority government, and ensuring that the NDP would influence any cabinet decision.

If the 1960s were about unconditional free-spiritedness - about the folly of doing something just because it was impulsive, fashionable, and ostensibly "free," the relative dullness of the 1970s led individuals to step behind the curtain, bored and looking for a new buzz. The headline in Tuesday's Globe and Mail read, "PM RUNS INTO THUNDER, BROKEN HARNESS, PUZZLING QUESTIONS," with far less ardor than when Trudeau only had to reveal a tuft of chest hair or sniff a rose to get the nation's pants wet. According to Sally Gibson, Trudeau visited Centre Island in 1968 for a Metro Liberal Party picnic, when he or a Metro Liberal Party picnic, where, according to Sally Gibson, he "shook hands with the faithful, danced with Miss Toronto, planted kisses on willing cheeks, and was adorned with two leis." He was jeered by protestors along the same shoreline a few years later, in 1971, for refusing to recognize the rights of island people.

The Prime Minister's weekend had begun in Brockville - no story would ever be worth telling with that kind of start, P.E.T. might have thought - and even if he'd performed his duties with a kind of natural aplomb (opening a military pageant, presenting the legion with a flag that had flown on the Peace Tower), there was no hiding the fact that, where he'd once performed these acts with dazzle and snap, Trudeau, he argued, shouldn't have been forced to engage in the kind of glad-handing stunts preferred by lesser politicians, even if he knew they were important. Still, given the precariousness of his party's hold on power - popular support for the Liberals had dwindled, and the country had grown cynical of Trudeau's Machiavellian leadership and air of political divinity - it may not have mattered what kinds of stunts or ceremonies he was forced to endure. It couldn't have been fun for Canada's leader to stand in shit-deep fields tickling babies, judging prized hogs, or doing whatever else the podunks of Brockville demanded.

Pierre Trudeau and Gordon Lightfoot had been the golden era's glittering hood ornaments since 1968. Both had given their countries a feeling of identity about the same period. If Trudeaumania had given way to novelty songs about sideburns and "fuddle duddle," Lightfoot's music was mostly heard on kitchen and cabin radios throughout his ascension. While the Prime

Minister reshaped Canada's notion of a leader, Lightfoot was its first natural-born star, redefining its sound by doing something few musicians had done before: referencing Canadian locations and events in songs that were as melodious and engaging as anything on the charts. And, if one of Trudeau's legacies was the development of an intellectual and cultural divide between Canada and the United States, Lightfoot was the first singer to achieve popular approbation in Canada before becoming famous in the United States.

But, if Trudeau lit Canada like a match to a firecracker's fuse, what remained after the light of EXPO and Montreal's Olympic victory was a country pawing its way through a cloud of stale smoke. The uncertainty of Trudeau's government symbolized the end of Canada's golden age, and there was anger and hostility against a leader who'd had too much, too soon, and too often in 1972.

Trudeau was slogging through the gloomy fields of Prince Edward County under gray skies and pouring rain during the week of July 10-16, while Lightfoot stayed hidden in his apartment to deal with Bell's palsy. Still, as the PM prepared to fire a 212-year-old cannon in yet another ceremonial gesture aimed to gain unwinnable votes, the old titfucker demonstrated that he was still alive. "At the start of Saturday's military pageant in Prescott, the master of ceremonies asked reporters and photographers to stand to the side and thirty feet away for safety reasons when Trudeau fired the cannon," according to CP. After a long wait, the Prime Minister made the following announcement: "The Prime Minister requests that the press take their positions in front of the cannon."

Francis had obtained funds from Trudeau's administration to operate her hostel, which assisted those who were traveling, hitchhiking, or in need of a place to stay. It was held near Clear Lake, with many sleeping tents and a cooking tent. "It was a twenty-four-hour operation, and we'd give out food as a form of hospitality," Francis explained. "That was also part of the funding; providing enough money to buy food to feed whoever came to a halt there." I had the idea after seeing Pierre Elliott Trudeau deliver a speech at the Kapuskasing airport. At the time, I was in high school, and everyone was chanting and screaming for him. 'You should all be traveling; you should see the world,' he added in his speech. We need to examine what other people are doing and how they live in order to understand who we are and what we do.' He informed us that traveling the world would provide us with a higher education than attending school. My mum still blames Trudeau for my dropping out of university."

Francis was content with her life in the north, but she felt she needed to see more of the province. "That summer of '72, someone told us about the Mariposa Folk Festival, and we decided to go," she recalled. "In the middle of the night, we drove down in a 1968 Camaro. It took eight hours. People were doing a lot of MDA back then, and I believe I purchased my hit from a vendor in the crafts area. It was extremely covert, but everyone knew how and where to get it."

Like Jean Francis, Gordon Flagler – twenty years old and living in Ottawa – worked at a youth hostel, in Carleton, where, he said, "there were lots of us on the payroll, and the whole thing was subsidized. We had four hundred people staying there every night. It cost fifty cents for dinner and breakfast and a place to sleep. The government also paid for buses that went out to the highway at night and picked up hitchhikers who couldn't get a ride. They brought them to us overnight, and came and picked them up the next morning, taking them back to the highway. In the late sixties and early seventies, everybody – well, every young person I knew – had a cool job created by the Trudeau government. I was within one application of getting a job driving an old hippie bus across Canada with a nurse to help people hitchhiking coast-to-coast."

Flagler also remembered something called the Le Dain Commission, an endeavor bankrolled by the Liberals to examine whether or not pot was dangerous. He said that the government had started an experimental farm near Carleton where they grew dope, and, one night, a few guys came into the hostel with bags full of pot. They'd crossed the river and harvested the stuff and no one had found out or even cared. These other friends of mine had it better than anyone. Their summer job was to go out to Rockcliffe airport at night, get stoned, and drive a bunch of cars around on the runways to measure the effects of marijuana on driving. This was the summer of 1971. A big part of Trudeau's message was 'Anything is possible.' We bought into it big time."

Flagler remembered going to see Crowbar play in 1971 in Stewart Park in Perth. "All of the politicians were around – guys in suits in their sixties and seventies standing next to their wives – and there was their leader in the middle – Pierre – wearing a cool buckskin jacket with his wife, Maggie, looking beautiful in a long gypsy dress. Maggie and Pierre were hanging out near the river listening to the band when a couple of freaks in a canoe rowed past them holding a big sign that said LEGALIZE MARIJUANA. Sometimes, people don't believe these stories, but they're true. I was there. I saw it happen."

It would be wrong to cast Trudeau as a music junkie, but there's no ignoring that his leadership had a direct effect on music in Canada. For the first time, musicians were treated the way poets and playwrights had been. They were recognized for their creativity and importance in a country once dominated by more traditional "artists." Having Canada's head of state attend rock shows was a huge boost for the players and their industry, and it says something that Trudeau's default tastes leaned to a band as outrageous as Crowbar, who were as known for their unpretentious and cartoonish live shows as for songs like.

Once, Roly Greenway of Crowbar was on stage at the Royal York Hotel with the prime minister – "I think we were getting a gold record for 'Oh, What a Feeling!' " – and he remembered telling a story to the crowd about the time the band played the PM's rally at Maple Leaf Gardens. Afterwards, Trudeau turned to him and said, "I don't know how you remembered that. You guys are always so fucking stoned." This frankness was part of Trudeau's appeal, said Roly. "He had a mouth on him. But he spoke like you and me. He was one of the guys," he added. "He got into our music because of Margaret, who used to come to see us play in Vancouver. We didn't gig there a lot, but when we did, she'd be front and center. She'd come in with a bunch of big burly guys, and she'd tell them,

'Lay off the band; they're okay.' We got to know each other pretty well. After we became popular, she brought Trudeau out, and we got to know him, too. Once, we were playing in Perth on a raft in the middle of the river. After our set, Sonny (Bernardi) and Kelly (Jay) went over to where Pierre and Maggie were standing. We'd been given a letter to pass on to him by the mayor of Hamilton, but, earlier in the day, we'd steamed it open, rolled two joints, and put them inside. He used to pass everything on to his staff, but when they gave him the envelope, they said, 'You might wanna keep what's inside for yourself.' He opened it up, took out the letter, and gave it to his staff. The envelope, he put in his pocket. Afterwards, we tried fitting a crowbar over his head – a kind of rock and roll coronation, I guess – but it wouldn't go. So Maggie came over and she slid it on. She knew how to do it, just so. Later on, the press wanted to know which of us had hooked up with Maggie, and when they asked, we all pointed at each other. She was my friend. She was just a nice, happy-go-lucky girl. It's too bad that it didn't work out. I liked both of them a lot. It's not often that you can describe the leader of your country in one word, but with Maggie and Trudeau, it would be *fun*."

As Trudeau drove home from Prescott, police and troops patrolled the countryside around Prince Edward County. Gaston Lambert, a twenty-two-year-old escaped convict, had buried himself in a mound of hay in the Newbury brothers' barn, waiting for the deep night to come before proceeding to who knows where. The stench of the animals replaced the foul stench of prison - ass and smoke and musk - and while he'd been able to at least manage his time inside by carrying a shiv in his pant leg or forming an alliance with the Newfies or trading Export A Green Deaths for other privileges, hiding in that barn reminded him how little control he had over the outside world, let alone the natural world, which went its own fucking way. When she saw him enter the barn, one of the cows yelled angrily, but the beasts quickly calmed down. The hay had dried out, and the ground was hard. Lambert wished to sleep, but his adrenalin was pumping. He thought he heard noises outside. A slow-moving pair of boots. Still, it could have been the beginning of the lunacy. Paranoia as a fugitive. That was something he'd heard could happen.

David McTaggart peered into the gorgeous emptiness on Tuesday, attempting to quantify his own insanity. It was soon after daybreak in the South Pacific, and his boat, the Vega, a 41-foot ketch, was slicing across the water. If his new home in New Zealand had forced him to fight to recall his history - years earning lucrative development contracts, national badminton championships, and a childhood life roaming the forests of British Columbia - being on the edge of the earth appeared to make everything else meaningless. The seas were calm, and the sun was getting orange fat on the horizon. McTaggart pondered putting on the radio and broadcasting a message to the entire world, but he changed his mind. Silence. He'd take advantage of it while he could.

Lambert heard footsteps approaching. They were massive, trampling the grass in front of the barn. They sounded terrible to him because he was weak and hungry and filthy and terrified, like something out of a terrifying children's book: tethered to a beast sharp-toothed and dark-furred, great-pawed and drooling. Lambert became terrified. He scurried out the back door and landed on his stomach, shimmying across the parched grass like an amphibian. He wished and hoped until he came to a shallow gully about a hundred feet from the barn. He rolled onto his back and listened while holding his breath. For a long time, there was only stillness, which was unsettling. Then the Newbury brothers arrived, looming over the sky's constellations. One of the brothers was holding a huge stick, while the other instructed Lambert to stand up. Lambert used to be a powerful, honorable man: left defense, iron spine, and hands the size of cinder bricks. He and his uncle once cleared an entire stand of black spruce by swinging axes and chopping cordwood, then retiring in their sleeping bags after dark and awakening six hours later to do it again. Lambert, on the other hand, had to leave the country and had softened. He met this guy and that guy and this guy and that guy in the city, and it felt like the best prospects were usually the ones with the most risk. "Take a seat. Begin walking." Lambert peed himself while lying down. "Stand up!" Lambert sprang to his feet. His feet were swollen and his groin was damp. "Stop. In opposition to that tree. "He turned around.." He spun around. "I'm wet," he admitted. "Stick him, Ray," one of the men said. Ray stabbed him. He pressed the long, pointed, crooked branch against Lambert's lower back. "I'm fucking dripping wet." He smacked Lambert with the stick until it hurt. "There, I can hear 'em," one of the men remarked. "About time," the other said. There are twenty-five cops. Lambert was soaked in pee as he stood against the tree. They'd know what had happened as soon as they saw him.

Dope there's dope go get 'em cries the voice inside the head of the ohio cop who finds himself suddenly surrounded by kids who have grown fangs and claws as their stoned summertime engine-work muscle rises to pull off his visor and then another cop's visor and before you know it it's vancouver all over again and here we are the stones on their exile tour trundling and trundling and trundling on. Cops are being killed. Below, officers are warped. Cops are stumbling backwards, and youngsters are writhing around, but after a while they don't know what to do, and furthermore, Stevie Wonder is playing: brap brap brap brap on that bizarre keyboard thing. Even though he can't see the carnage raging through the bowl, he can feel the legs of his keyboard wheeze as the stage rocks just so with surging bodies trying to get out of or into the conflict. Chip Monck goes on stage, grabs the mic, and instructs everyone to stop, even Stevie, though he'll resume as soon as more cops arrive at the fallen cops, where they headlock the naughty kids into the paddy wagon and yell pigs pigs. Pigs are in charge of the planet. Stevie will perform a song from his latest album, Talking Book. In 1972, he would open for the Stones in Ohio before heading to Canada. Strange fucking job.

LETTER IN WHICH I ASK YOU ABOUT TRACK AND FIELD AND ROCK AND ROLL

JOHN WILFRED LOARING

John Wilfred Loaring was one of Canada's early track stars, capturing silver in the 400m at the 1936 Olympics. Loaring, who had rheumatic illness as a child in Winnipeg but survived, also raced the relay. In the semi-final relay heat, he received the baton ahead of his teammate, Rudolph Harbig, who would go on to set world records in the 400 and 800 a few years later. Loaring slowed down during the heat so that Harbig could pass him and win in front of his compatriots. Canada would proceed to the final regardless, and it seemed like the right thing to do in a bygone era of sporting gallantry.

Loaring completed his final examinations early in his final year of university to be among the first batch of Royal Canadian Naval Volunteer Radar Officers on loan to the British during World War II, leaving Canada in April 1940. His warship was deployed in September 1940 to pick up civilian survivors of a destroyed liner. Here's another thing. This one, I made up:

ORILLIA TIMES, MAY 24TH, 1952 BY DONALD RIVARD

Gord, you like singing, but you also enjoyed athletics (did I mention how great that makes you appear?). Let me ask you: was it the smell of the field at 8 a.m.? The scent of wet earth pushed out by the clover, and how your runners felt bouncing across the new spring grass as you left the scent of your parents' kitchen in the morning, the coffee boiled and eggs frying in the pan, Mom still in her nightgown, Father fixed for Wagg's, where he would go to work every morning for thirty years, becoming manager, middle class, and prosperous, all things considered. Your legs' hair undoubtedly bristled at the touch of the air, which still held a tingle of the ice frozen in up the bay, the weight of summer still months away.

Running across the field in your new shoes for the first time gave your feet vitality, and you felt like you were running faster than ever. You were alone at first, then everyone else arrived: Scoot, Rocky, Mouse, Whelan, The Mole, Branch, Skerf, Jones (some of those names are made up; some are from Collins' book). Whelan might have said, "They don't give out ribbons for showing up first, you know," and you tried to smile at your friend, but you couldn't, and he understood since he was your friend. Later, as you walked to the starting line, you might have tightened your fists thinking about John Loaring, the closest thing the Dominion had to a track star, how he'd raced to catch the German running for Hitler, lost him at the finish line, then bowed his head before telling his coaches, "Let the foul ride; let it be pure victory or nothing."

The gun cracked.

You ran.

So there you have it: high school. Everyone must go through it. I'm not sure what it was like for you as a musician - I can speculate, and I'll tell you what I think I know in a moment - but it was like being lost in space for me. The universe. I was hanging out with three other buddies who were into New Wave. Do you understand what the term means, Gord? Carol Pope is a woman. The Spoons are a band. Synthesizers. The cops. Anyway, my three buddies and I were into New Wave, when everyone else was into anything else. They enjoyed disco and hard rock, which I did as well, but hard rock was too difficult to perform, at least on guitar. You see, New Wave guitar was perfect for me.

We did a couple gigs downtown before being asked to perform at one of our school dances in Grade Thirteen. The offer caught us off guard because we didn't think anyone cared or was paying attention to us other than screaming out "freak!" or "weirdo!" in the hallway. I believe the professors noticed, since one of them and a couple students from the student council invited us to play. We'd played at a high school party in Scarborough before, miles from where we lived on the other side of Toronto, and gave out 45s as we crossed the dark dance floor; teenagers shot the platters at our heads as we crossed the dark dance floor. We feared the worst at our school. But as soon as we started playing, the other kids realized we weren't too bad, so they quit the nonsense and began dancing. Gord, it was complete Cotton Candy, Disney crap, a true accomplishment. We graduated a few months later, and while high school still suffered, we graduated on top.

In high school, a lot of kids rebelled, and playing in a New Wave band was our revolt. Some kids become involved with drugs, black magic, vampires, knives, bisexuality, conservatism, veganism, paganism, plush toys, subway tagging, German theater, wacky hairstyles, cell-porn, protesting, hacking computers, blowing jobs, or becoming pregnant. There are several methods for children growing up in the twenty-first century to rebel, but the concept of rebellion becomes more predictable with each generation. If a child does not rebel these days, parents become concerned; however, in the 1950s, which marked the beginning of North American adolescent rebellion, or at least the popularization or perhaps marketing of adolescent rebellion, to be a rebel was to be truly bad, as opposed to today's kids who go to the mall, get a twenty-dollar tattoo as a sign of independence, and believe they are Damian Abraham or Jenny Mechanic.

So you accepted the uncool. That is most likely what makes you cool. But here's something I'm not sure about. In your high school yearbook, under "Pet Peeves," you put "Squares." But you were a complete jerk. Were you being ironic and funny? Or were you simply perplexed? I've known a number of extremely amazing musicians who moved through the world savant-like, with no sense of cool or otherwise, but this can't be your time. It was the 1950s.

Cool was everything, cool was everything. After all, you were just a few years later playing Top Forty - rock and roll and pop - with your mate Whelan in Ontario's lodges and taverns. Perhaps the message you were sending to people - to your friends, to your parents, to the world - by doing this and singing barbershop was that you were Gordon Lightfoot, and you didn't care. You would if no one else in Orillia was singing jazz, show tunes, or barbershop. No one in Canada was singing about Canada a few years later, but you were. And when folk music went electric in the 1960s, you avoided drums and fuzz guitar like they were hep A and B. You played right before Dylan's set at Newport, the one where he turned electric. You were introduced by Peter, Paul, and Mary before your set - I imagine them sandaled in flowered caftans, arms bouquets with tin whistles and recorders, one of them snuggling an autoharp - but not many people remember it because of Dylan's performance, which left his long-time fans in tatters, many of them demanding an apology from their young bard. Following that, folkies let their autoharps spring against the floor, their herbal tea oil-lamped utopia of cartoon dragons and Castenedian poetry buried beneath The Band's muddy colossus and Dylan's electric depravity. Nobody knows how you felt, but over the next six to eight months, while every Tunesman, Merry Wanderer, and Laughing Dolphin Quintet was tacking music stores with ads seeking bassists and drummers, you silently returned home to concentrate on your tunes. Perhaps it was an act of defiance, perhaps not. If Dylan's new sound continued to vibrate in the ear chambers of those who heard it like an insane laughing monster, you refused any inclination to modify. Dylan's new sound may have given birth to the Mamas and the Papas - just saying their names makes my stomach turn, Gord - but you went out and got two talented and inventive sidemen: Red Shea and John Stockfish. It turned out to be just enough change.

When you were asked to fill out the area of your yearbook labeled "Probable Destination," you wrote, "Diaper washer at Wagg's." I believe you were joking here. Still, I believe you were saying, "I am Gordon Lightfoot." Nobody is going to stop me from doing whatever the fuck I want."

WEDNESDAY, JULY 12TH

The sky continued to bubble and hiss, foam and spit on Wednesday. The globe was in a state of vertical upheaval, from top to bottom, from clouds to dirt. Two Starfighter planes collided in mid-air over Brussels that morning. The planes were destroyed, with one collapsing into a home and the other nose-diving into a farmer's field. Surprisingly, both pilots bailed and no one was seriously harmed. The calamity struck abruptly, like the batting of a dragonfly's wings, whereas the drama in the sky over the United States was drawn out and, in the end, far less remarkable.

Melvin Fisher was primarily to blame. His strategy was meant to work, and it did for a little while. But then awful stuff happened; bad stuff you don't want or need, especially when there's already a lot of bad stuff going on. Melvin was a house painter in need of funds. He was divorced, had six children, and was in debt. Debts that are not paid. He also had charges pending in Texas, the lowest level of swindling, and no chances for employment, at least not in Norman, Oklahoma. He despised painting houses. He despised dressing up enormous houses for affluent guys who referred to the crew as "ladies" and wanted him to know how much he was getting ripped off by hiring such wrinkled hippies and losers. Melvin's wife had stripped him naked in divorce court. You know how that went because the judge was a woman. Melvin believed he could make money by doing what many others had done, even though it had rarely worked. D.B. Cooper had done it and then vanished. A few months later, Palestinian terrorists carried out the attack at the Munich Olympics before fleeing to safety. Perhaps it was the sense of adventure that piqued his interest. Perhaps it was an opportunity to demonstrate to his ex-wife that he could accept responsibility once and for all. Perhaps it was the power that comes with holding a dozen strangers' lives in your hands and returning them to land unscathed. He was not going to use bullets. That would be incorrect. He thought to himself, "Jesus Christ, I'm not a maniac." I'm not a murderer.

The events of Wednesday night were equally the fault of Michael Green and Lulseged Tesfa, though Green and Tesfa were considerably worse to their passengers. Green and Tesfa were unrepentant after everything went wrong, with Melvin sobbing uncontrollably in the judge's chambers and excusing himself every ten minutes to vomit once the reality set in that he would be spending the rest of his life trying not to get stabbed or ass-fucked in prison. They were thugs, and they understood what they were getting themselves into. Green and Tesfa pistol-whipped and crushed the pelvis of the National Airlines jet's co-pilot while Melvin flashed an unloaded gun, which he later handed to a hostess. They also shot the flight engineer, Gerald Beaver, before turning off the cabin lights, turning off the air conditioning, and demanding that the jet stay in the air indefinitely.

was doing pretty soon after the American Airlines plane took off, but tried seeing the plan through in an effort to prove something to himself, although damned if he knew what that was. His original idea was to fly from Oklahoma City to Fort Worth, get the cash and a parachute, and then jump to wherever the wind blew him. But a storm raged across the south and the plane had to be diverted home. At first, Melvin thought it was a ploy, but the skies outside told a different story. Upon landing, authorities brought him a bag of money and a parachute, but this was only after Melvin agreed to release all fifty-seven passengers, as well as three stewardesses.

Green and Tesfa, on the other hand, kept their passengers hostage for nine hours in the air without AC or electricity. People fainted. Others screamed and called out to their captors. The 727 circled above the Philadelphia airport as the hijackers negotiated with FBI agents on the ground, landing only after the plane's fuel dropped too low to continue. Once on the tarmac, the pilot escaped through a window. All 113 passengers were released and the hijackers were transferred, along with four stewardesses, the co-pilot, and the flight engineer, to another aircraft, which, according to the Associated Press, "flew over Dallas, then Houston, then swung south over the Gulf of Mexico, eventually landing at Lake

Jackson." One of the stewardesses fled from the plane, and then Green and Tesfa, despite having been given their ransom, surrendered; bond would later be set at one million dollars each. Hanging in the clouds, Melvin Fisher counted his money in the cockpit of the 727. When he got to the bottom of the bag, he saw that his hands were stained purple from the marked bills, which amounted to less than half of what he'd demanded: $200,000. Melvin asked the nice flight attendant if she wouldn't mind opening the rear door of the plane so he might jump out. Certainly, she might have said, twirling on her heels. Reports confirm that Fisher had the plane circle for two more hours as he straddled his parachute and worked up the courage to fall to earth. But he couldn't. Instead, he told the pilot to land, and the next thing he knew he was bawling into the flat of his hands as the charges were read from the bench. In the end, it's what people had always said about him: even with a weapon, the guy couldn't fight his way out of a paper bag.

Pioneer 10 kept traveling, fuelled by plutonium and coming closer to Jupiter. Scientists sipped coffee and tracked it daily, then hourly, then in ten-minute increments, hoping that anything so small might avoid being destroyed by entities forty times its size and traveling at unfathomable speeds. NASA had produced two gold-anodized aluminum plaques designed by Carl Sagan, Linda Sagan, and Frank Drake months before the spacecraft's launch, which they fastened to the spacecraft's bus. Each plaque displayed "Earth's place in the solar system from which it came; a silhouette of the vehicle itself; when it was launched; a diagram representing fourteen pulsars that were arranged to show a scientifically literate being where the home star of this system was located; and a naked man and a woman," according to William E. Burrows, author of This New Ocean. "The man's right hand was raised as a sign of peace," Burrows wrote. The woman stood motionless beside him." The author recalls that "the problem of showing naked people to American families confounded print and television media," and that "the Chicago Sun-Times reacted by airbrushing out the couple's genitals and her breasts." Outraged feminists objected to the woman being put slightly behind the guy, without having a hand up, and looking at him with obvious admiration, which they claimed amounted to subjugation. The outraged women alleged that the message that the male-dominated, macho NASA planned to send to the farthest reaches of the universe was that their own sex was subordinate." Burrows writes that "the uproar over the plaque said as much about life on Earth as what it depicted," but NASA couldn't have cared less about social or political decorum as the little spaceship cruised towards its objective. They claimed that it had nothing to do with politics or gender. It has to do with space. It had to do with humanity. It had to do with the universe. More coffee, please.

David McTaggart scratched his beard while floating alone in the earth's soup millions of kilometers beneath the small chugging spacecraft, waiting for it all to go to hell. He had an idea while doing this: he would nickname the Vega. It would now be known as Greenpeace III, after the new environmental organization they'd founded back home, and as the boat swished across the blue-green waters towards the French South Pacific, 125 miles east of the Cook Islands, McTaggart finally felt like he was a part of something big, something that, one day, would consume the world's attention. The captain informed Radio Rarotonga that he had arrived at the nuclear test zone, just beyond the Mururoa Atoll. He stated that if they were going to blow shit up, they would also blow him up. The boat gently rocked. Its captain sat in silence, waiting for an answer.

On Wednesday, police and troops used dogs, rifles, and netting to sweep the fields and ditches near Kingston, while the fugitive convicts sought to blend in. Thomas Smith, one of them, cuddled up between two trees and fantasized about smoking. Smith enjoyed smoking. He enjoyed the delicious, hot burn of the tobacco against the chill of his throat, and how the nicotine entered his bloodstream as if it were swinging from a rope, wearing a big feathered hat and boots and swishing a sword through the air. The buzz tingled his shoulders and the base of his neck, and the cylinder sat perfectly weighted between his fingers. He was obsessed with the thought of smoking as food and smoking as an activity, and it was all he could think about as he hid in the nettled and scratchy bush outside of Napanee. While freedom meant easy pussy and fast cars and Playboys and buckets of booze and the warmth of sons and daughters and Mom's food cooked all day then served with a bottle of beer, cooler ice sliding down its neck as it warmed in their hands, it meant smokes burned one after the other as he approached the front window crowded with Spiderman dolls and black joke gum and Kingston Canadians pennants and lava lamps and Apollo 11 modeling kits. Bozo the clown sags in the middle of the tangle of kitsch. Smith pushed through the door, a little bell ringing beneath the frame. He requested du Mauriers. There are three packs. "Three?" the old man behind the counter asked, looking at Smith, then out the window. "Why not four?" "Three," Smith said before rethinking. "No. "Four, please." "How about a carton?" said the elderly gentleman. Smith said that he will buy a carton later. The old man reviewed his inventory and then indicated he'd have to go back to the store to get a new carton. "No problem, just take your time." Smith was in a terrific mood. The elderly gentleman had not even noticed what he was wearing. He hadn't sniffed him or assessed him. He was, after all, quite old. The man reappeared, carrying three du Maurier red decks. He piled them up on the counter. The door opened, and the bell rang again. Constable Goyer went over the specifics of Smith's arrest with the reporter from the Star before telling him, "You know, what caught that guy was his yearning for cigarettes."

On Wednesday, it was announced at a reception at the Sutton Place Hotel in Toronto that Canada would put its title as the world's greatest hockey nation on the line in an eight-game "Summit" series against a Soviet Union squad. The announcement was made while Peter Appleyard played his mallets and Ginni Grant (of the Phil Nimmons band) sang the new Team Canada anthem ("Team Canada, we're with you all the way!"), which the Toronto Star described as "folk rock." They also stated that "food, shrimp, scallops, and egg rolls were plentiful, and the models were more delicious than the food." As the names of the players were read, Harry Sinden drank his Molson Extra Old Stock and watched what looked like a goddamned fashion show on the goddamned Sutton Place hotel stage as two dozen grown men - hockey players, professionals, all of them - walked up there laughing and smiling in their white ties and plaid jackets while the goddamned photographers asked them to pose like goddamned fags in a goddamned fag parade. The only thing the goddamned writers wanted to talk about was Bobby Hull - Hull this, Hull that - and whether they were going to let him play, even though he'd named him to the goddamned team, which is what Harry had said he would do all along. "We strove for balance; offense and defense; finesse and aggressiveness," Sinden told Proudfoot. And, while the goddamned experts wondered why this player or that player wasn't named - there were no Penguins, Kings, Seals, or Blues on the team - he could have named thirty-five other players and it still wouldn't be easy beating the goddamned Russians because, sure, they were strange and their equipment was shit, and they had weird names and flowerpot helmets, and they came from a dark and horrible place far, far away, but, je Following the introduction, models dressed in Team Canada sweaters and black miniskirts worked the room, selling beer and champagne, but Harry was unable to partake. Politics. Owners. Hull, and his goddamned new contract with the goddamned WHA. Whose idea was it for him to coach this goddamned team in the first place?

The French were enraged. They'd spent months trying to get the money through the system before rigging the detonators, clearing the atoll as best they could, and putting everything in place to properly assess the impacts of their blasts. Because that tiny Canadian crap McTaggart was where he was - downwind yet anchored, according to the formal international water boundaries - he would be ripped apart by the frightening Day-Glo of the massive nuclear bomb. The testing could only continue if McTaggart and his Greenpeace vessel were evacuated. The French set about doing so.

After putting an ad for next Tuesday's Rare Earth concert into the cart machine, someone named Jungle Johnny, Cool Mo, Dave the

Dragon, or Electric Earl spent the better part of Wednesday afternoon spinning around in his chair until he came face to face with a wooden rack containing the Top Forty singles of July 10, 1972, hung on dowels. The deejays debated whether to play "Layla" or "Lean on Me" or "Where Is the Love?" or "Long Cool Woman (In a Black Dress)" by The Hollies, the catchy T. After their first drummer, John Rutsey, questioned the ethics of the musicians' union, the band was forced to do the gig. Rush was forced to play a so-called trust-fund gig at the lunatic asylum as a result of the union's response. "They took us to these ten-foot high barricaded doors," said crew member Ian Grandy. [We knocked on the door], and a man with half his head melted tried to get out before being tackled to the ground. The event drew sixty attendees, including one man who thought he was Elvis. They positioned seven elderly ladies directly in front of the PA speakers. They were catatonic and unblinking." Geddy Lee, for one, recalls another detail. "One of the inmates tried escaping with us during load out."

In between playing singles from the singles chart and album sides by Pink Floyd, Steely Dan, and Led Zeppelin, the deejays talked film, or at least movies with a musical connection: The Harder They Come by Jimmy Cliff, with its groundbreaking soundtrack that introduced people to reggae artists other than Bob Marley; Gordon Parks' Superfly, whose Curtis Mayfield-written theme song had infused summer radio; Fritz the Cat, the first animated film to receive an X-rating; Lady Sings the Blues, starring Diana Ross; and Sounder, whose cast included a dust-swept and dobro-playing Taj Mahal. They might have also discussed other films from 1972: Ned Beatty's feral performance in Deliverance; Shelley Winter's dog-paddle for daylight in The Poseidon Adventure; Tarkovsky's space-epic, Solaris; Woody Allen being chased around by an enormous breast in Everything You Always Wanted to Know About Sex (But Were Afraid to Ask); Cabaret's transexual character; Ben, starring Michael Jackson and thousands of rats; Boxcar Bertha, Martin Scorsese's

What's Up, Doc?, directed by Peter Bogdanovich and starring Ryan O'Neal and Barbra Streisand, is the 1972 film I remember the most. It was the first mature film I'd ever seen, therefore I remember it fondly. It didn't have any animated woodchucks, caped superheroes, or Old Yeller animals in it; simply caper laughter and minimal sexual innuendo that passed my parents' scrutiny.

Mariposa '72, in Goddard's perspective, wasn't recognized as an important event until after the fact. "Actually, it wasn't until I sat down to write about the event that I realized what had just happened," he admitted. "We didn't realize history was in the making until it was made," said Bruce Cole, who was recruited to shoot the weekend.

Goddard feels that the festival would have had a greater immediate impact if it had occurred a few years after the events of September 13, 1969, at Varsity Stadium, which he claims left Flower Power bloodied and lifeless. There, John Lennon and his new wife, the diminutive and enigmatic Yoko Ono, made their debut with their new band, the Plastic Ono Band.

The festival was produced by John Brower and Kenny Walker, who had just a few months previously staged another mega-show, the two-day Toronto Pop Festival. Brower and Walker lost the confidence of their two key sponsors, department store heirs George and Thor Eaton, due to low early ticket sales, and the Revival was almost canceled. However, California garage-rock entrepreneur and producer Kim Fowley, who was in Toronto to promote the event with announcer and Sunset Strip figure Rodney Bingenheimer, proposed that Brower invite John and Yoko to emcee the festival to pique people's attention.

If Mariposa was a kind of easy paradise where musicians and fans could commune on an island, the Revival was held in the smoldering center of the grimy city. A police cruiser was attacked and rocked by fifty kids at one point, while inside the stadium, fans staged garbage battles and others freaked out on acid and PCP. The show itself was a mixed bag. According to the Star's Melinda McCracken, singer and guitarist Bo Diddley was dressed in a "dark red metallic suit" and aroused the crowd of 20,000 by "stomping around the stage" before closing his act by collapsing to his knees and wailing. The Chicago Transit Authority took the stage next, followed by the day's march of legends, which included a tired-looking and portly Gene Vincent, who was supported by the Alice Cooper Band and surrounded by Vagabond bikers standing arms crossed at the front of the stage. According to McCracken, Jerry Lee Lewis nearly ruined his instrument by "jumping up and down on the grand piano," while during Chuck Berry's concert ("he possessed an aura of slick vulgarity," observed McCracken), a group of fans tore off their clothes before being smeared with mustard by Bingenheimer. miniature Richard arrived with a huge show band and "a beautiful white suit covered in little one-inch mirrors." "Little Richard didn't care about the event being historic or anything," Goddard says. He just went out there and played. It was evident from the start that he wasn't about to be overshadowed by anyone, let alone a Beatle."

Three Toronto musicians were members of Chuck Berry's backing band, including Danny Taylor and Hugh Leggat of Nucleus, who created the foundation for Foot In Cold Water. Taylor and Leggat were invited to the event by Brower, who handled Nucleus alongside Shel Saffron, producer of the Amboy Dukes, and others. Taylor recalled, "Shel asked us early in the day if we wanted to back up Chuck Berry, and we said, 'Yeah, sure, whatever.'" We didn't think much of it because it seemed like an insane idea. Then, right before the show was set to begin, he said, 'Okay, you're on in a few minutes.'" Leggat recalled that "the bass player who was supposed to play with Chuck was shaking because he didn't know the tunes." But no one did. Chuck didn't travel with a band; he just picked up musicians in whatever place he was playing in. So I figured, shit, I didn't have anything to lose."

Leggat recalled the famed guitarist deliberately looking away from the band so they couldn't see his hands. "I couldn't figure out what key he was in, so I went over and asked him." He raised his hands, stopped whatever song we were playing, and announced to 20,000 people, 'The bass player here wants to know what key we're playing in!' He was playing with us. It wasn't until about a half-hour into the show that he relaxed into some mellow blues, and that's when it really started to click. When I looked over, there was my brother at the side of the stage. Jim Morrison was standing alongside him, gesticulating with his head. Jim asked for a drink from my brother's lengthy wineskin. He drank it all, and it flowed down the front of his T-shirt. The alcohol was loaded with homemade meth and three types of acid, but Jim didn't appear to mind. 'More! I want more!' he grabbed my brother.

Taylor recalls, "After the gig, we were sitting around in the dressing room." Hughie asked Chuck if he'd ever tried a Harvey's hamburger after he claimed he was hungry. 'What's that?' Chuck inquired, and Hugh responded. Chuck asked where he might buy one, and we informed him there was one across the street. So the two of us, along with Chuck Berry, who was still dressed for the stage in a paisley waistcoat and suit, crossed Bloor Street at St. George and ordered burgers." "I remember the guy who was flipping burgers asking Chuck if he wanted cheese on his," Leggat says. 'How much does that cost?' Chuck inquired. 'Five cents,' he said. "I don't want any cheese."

If Mariposa was a kind of easy paradise where musicians and fans could congregate on an island, the Revival was held in the scorching heart of the slum. At one point, fifty kids attacked and rocked a police cruiser, while inside the stadium, fans staged garbage battles and others freaked out on acid and PCP. The show itself was a bit of a mixed bag.The Chicago Transit Authority followed, followed by the day's march of legends, which included a tired-looking and portly Gene Vincent, who was supported by the Alice Cooper Band and surrounded by Vagabond bikers standing arms crossed at the front of the stage.

Three Toronto musicians were part of Chuck Berry's backing band, including Nucleus' Danny Taylor and Hugh Leggat, who laid the groundwork for Foot In Cold Water. Brower, who managed Nucleus alongside Shel Saffron, producer of the Amboy Dukes, and others, invited Taylor and Leggat to the gathering. "Shel asked us early in the day if we wanted to back up Chuck Berry, and we said, 'Yeah, sure, whatever.'" We didn't give it much thought because it seemed like a crazy idea. Then, just as the show was about to start, he said, 'Okay, you're on in a few minutes.'" According to Leggat, "the bass player who was supposed to play with Chuck was shaking because he didn't know the tunes." However, no one did. Chuck didn't travel with a band; he just picked up musicians wherever he played. So I figured, shit, I had nothing to lose."

Leggat remembers the legendary guitarist turning away from the band so they couldn't see his hands. "I couldn't figure out what key he was in, so I went over and asked him." He raised his hands, paused the performance, and said to 20,000 spectators, 'The bass player here wants to know what key we're playing in!'

Taylor recalls, "After the gig, we were sitting around in the dressing room. "Hughie inquired of Chuck whether he'd ever had a Harvey's hamburger after he claimed to be hungry. 'What is it?' Hugh answered Chuck's inquiry. Chuck inquired as to where he could purchase one, and we informed him that there was one across the street. So the two of us crossed Bloor Street at St. George, along with Chuck Berry, who was still dressed for the stage in a paisley waistcoat and suit, and got burgers." "I remember the guy who was flipping burgers asking Chuck if he wanted cheese on his," Leggat recalls. 'How much is that going to cost?' Chuck was curious. 'Five cents,' he explained. "I don't want any cheese."

"When Yoko came out of her bag," David Keshen, who was seated a few feet away from the stage, observed, "the look on Eric Clapton's face suggested that he just wanted to shrink away." "It's hard not to conclude that John Lennon hasn't saddled himself with an awkward, demanding, difficult, and weird partner - and co-leader - in his current musical enterprises," wrote the Star's other music reporter, Jack Batten, in his assessment of the event.During this time, Batten characterized Lennon as standing around with his hands in his jacket pockets, "looking like a man waiting for a very late streetcar."

Following the show, John and Yoko spoke to reporters from a wooden bench in a little bleak locker room in the stadium's bowels, which smelled like gym socks and old drains. "We are interested in exploring new sounds," Yoko told the audience. "John and I are disappointed that we did not see all of the performers who influenced The Beatles during the Rock and Roll Revival." Someone asked Yoko what was next as they snuck away into another room. She informed them that they were exhausted and were going to bed.

Mariposa '72 might not have happened if the Varsity Stadium show had not established Toronto as a place where the impossible was conceivable. Mariposa's stars were likely drawn to the city for the same reasons that Lennon was: a thriving music scene, entrepreneurs with access to the new money of old families, a generation of kids exposed to new sounds and styles, and a lack of the nonsense that usually accompanied such large-scale events. Furthermore, unlike Los Angeles, New York, or London, the metropolis was manageable in size, and at the time, Canada, or at least Toronto, possessed both familiarity and northern exoticism.

Years before, Toronto's image as a musical center had been built through a gig map that drew American blues and jazz musicians who were welcomed by Toronto while being unbookable in many parts of their own nation. During the 1967 CNE, their performance at the CHUM stage just inside the Princes' Gates sparked a riot that had to be put down by police on horseback. He was rock and roll girl candy at night and Latin, science, and algebra at school during the day.

Sebastian also performed in a country band at the Edison Hotel on Yonge Street, but he wasn't permitted to stay because he was underage. He used to sneak upstairs to Steele's Tavern, where Lightfoot played every night in the mid 1960s. The doorman let him stand near the entry, listening to the singer's low, resonant baritone float through the door, passing over him before getting lost in the steel wool of city traffic and pedestrians trampling down the bustling walkways. He'd arrive home late, sleep late, and then do it all over again.

The Lords of London were one of the busiest musical concerns in the city. They were the go-to opening act for prominent touring artists, and they opened for Jimi Hendrix and the Mothers of Invention just a few days apart in 1969. "When Hendrix showed up at the Gardens, we were smoking a joint," Angello recalls. He asked if he may have some, and we said fine, but he basically ruined it. He'd just crossed the border and was starving. I delivered the news that there wasn't really someplace to eat - there were no twenty-four-hour eateries in Toronto back then - so I said, 'Hey, let's just go to my parents' place. 'I'm sure my mother will cook us something.' That's exactly what we did. My mother awoke in the middle of the night and prepared a large spaghetti lunch for myself, my friends, and Hendrix's drummer. It was delectable. Before he died, I received an email from him in which he stated that, while he didn't remember much about touring with Hendrix, this was something he did. He remembers that night, as well as my mother's pasta."

The Lords of London were only one of several bands performing in the city. The Kensington Market and The Ugly Ducklings were two additional marquee rock performers with a soulful rage and determined musicianship, and whose millions of fans were among the first to be drawn to, and crazy about, local rock and roll. The

Paupers were another group. When individuals discuss The Paupers, they pause before attempting to describe the band's sound, then clarify that what they've said isn't nearly enough. Early electronic treatments and sound waves snaking through the tumult of a wildly thunderous band squeezed onto one of Yorkville's matchbox stages; a bass player, Denny Gerrard, whose solos were so intense and complicated that his fingers bled afterwards, and whom Geddy Lee cites as his first musical hero; songs that were epic and brave without being pretentious or silly; televisions that were occasionally destroyed at the end of sets; "The Paupers make impossible sounds with their instruments," observed Richard Goldstein of the Village Voice, "and it is all there, right before you, real." However, comprehending the band's magnificence is akin to staring into an overgrown and untended view. Fans admit that the band's raw strength was never adequately captured on record, leaving us with merely the outline of a story and a studiofied image of one of Canada's wildest, most emotive, and creative bands.

Sebastian also performed in a country band at the Edison Hotel on Yonge Street, but he wasn't permitted to stay because he was underage. He used to sneak upstairs to Steele's Tavern, where Lightfoot played every night in the mid 1960s. The doorman let him stand near the entry, listening to the singer's low, resonant baritone float through the door, passing over him before getting lost in the steel wool of city traffic and pedestrians trampling down the bustling walkways. He'd arrive home late, sleep late, and then do it all over again.

The Lords of London were one of the busiest musical concerns in the city. They were the go-to opening act for prominent touring artists, and they opened for Jimi Hendrix and the Mothers of Invention just a few days apart in 1969. "When Hendrix showed up at the Gardens, we were smoking a joint," Angello recalls. He asked if he may have some, and we said fine, but he basically ruined it. He'd just crossed the border and was starving. I delivered the news that there wasn't really someplace to eat - there were no twenty-four-hour eateries in Toronto back then - so I said, 'Hey, let's just go to my parents' place. 'I'm sure my mother will cook us something.' That's exactly what we did. My mother awoke in the middle of the night and prepared a large spaghetti lunch for myself, my friends, and Hendrix's drummer. It was delectable. Before he died, I received an email from him in which he stated that, while he didn't remember much about touring with Hendrix, this was something he did. He remembers that night, as well as my mother's pasta."

The Lords of London were only one of several bands performing in the city. The Kensington Market and The Ugly Ducklings were two additional marquee rock performers with a soulful rage and determined musicianship, and whose millions of fans were among the first to be drawn to, and crazy about, local rock and roll. The Paupers were another group. When individuals discuss The Paupers, they pause before attempting to describe the band's sound, then clarify that what they've said isn't nearly enough. Early electronic treatments and sound waves snaking through the tumult of a wildly thunderous band squeezed onto one of Yorkville's matchbox stages; a bass player, Denny Gerrard, whose solos were so intense and complicated that his fingers bled afterwards, and whom Geddy Lee cites as his first musical hero; songs that were epic and brave without being pretentious or silly; televisions that were occasionally destroyed at the end of sets; "The Paupers make impossible sounds with their instruments," observed Richard Goldstein of the Village Voice, "and it is all there, right before you, real." However, comprehending the band's magnificence is akin to staring into an overgrown and untended view. Fans admit that the band's raw strength was never adequately captured on record, leaving us with merely the outline of a story and a studiofied image of one of Canada's wildest, most emotive, and creative bands.

Canadian music found itself in the summer of 1972, with so many domestic stars making a mark in Canada and over the world, and CanCon pushed to its full legislative throttle. "It was as if country music was maturing," Roly Greenway recalls. "Trudeau's government had brought in CanCon, and we took advantage of it."

People don't realize how difficult it was before there was any radio action. People didn't embrace Canadian musicians as much as they do now, and as a result, you sometimes found yourself playing in the worst venues, clubs where you had to puke and show your razor blade before entering. Six evenings a week, we would back up strippers. We were known as The Ascots, and we did cover songs. We once heard that Ronnie Hawkins was holding auditions to find a group of players to replace The Band, so we'd play until one a.m. in London, drive down to Hamilton, arrive at three, rehearse or audition until seven, and then drive back to London and sleep in a bed that wasn't always a bed. It was just a floor. We were living above the Hawk's Nest - Ronnie's Yonge Street club - when we got the job, subsisting on one hot dog per day. Ronnie was cheap, and he reasoned that if he starved us, we'd be his, which was often the case because we didn't want to go back to the strip clubs. Ronnie used to fine you $5 if you stepped on his mike cords. We once did two sold-out nights at New York's Fillmore East, opening for Joe Cocker and The Stone Poneys, and he handed us each $20. We'd been living with his sister on Long Island, and he told us, 'Well, you know, I've got to pay my sister for all of the food she's been giving you,' which was mostly hot dogs and canned beans. That's why succeeding on our own was so significant for us. Nobody could have predicted the effect and significance of a popular song. I recall driving up to a show in Oshawa in 1972 and seeing all of these folks crammed around the pavement. I assumed there had been some sort of terrible accident. They were, nevertheless, fans. They recognized our song and were overjoyed to see us. I recall the expressions on everyone's faces. We felt like rock stars."

According to Finkelstein, it was not only CanCon that transformed things in the 1970s, but also the 1971 reduction in the drinking age. "Drinking changed the tastes of the average Toronto kid." It's one of the reasons why Rush was able to find an audience. At that moment, you had to be loud, but you couldn't be preachy because everyone was too busy drinking and having a wonderful time." However, not everyone supported the Maple Law: "Lightfoot, of course, was opposed to it because he didn't need it, and he felt that it would threaten his domination of Canadian radio," remembers Al

Mair, Lightfoot's former manager. I spoke in favor of it at the public hearings, but not without some trepidation. I didn't inform Gord until I was finished since I knew he wouldn't approve."

If the summer of '72 was a moment when Canadian bands were receiving the advantages of a new musical enlightenment, it wasn't long before the contradictions of CanCon were apparent like traplines in melting snow. But when I got my A&M contract in 1977, I embarked on a cross-country promotional tour. People were forced to accept whatever record corporations were putting out as a result of the Maple Law. I and an A&R person once offered a radio programmer our new record. He looked at it and instantly threw it on his desk, where it skittered across the floor and into the garbage pail. "Ah, fuck, no more CanCon!" I remember the programmer moaning loud while it was still skittering.

LETTER IN WHICH YOU PLAY A RESORT AND WE MEET A VENTRILOQUIST

Hey, Gord. Here's another newspaper clipping. I made this one up, too:

ADVERTISEMENT FROM ORILLIA TIMES, JUNE 7, 1956

Sully and Silas, stars of the 1954 Canadian National Exhibition and the Wayne and Shuster Comedy Hour, will be performing all month in the Manitou Room of the Big Chief Lodge, Monday through Friday. The musical stylings of local up-and-comers The Two-Timers, singing tunes from Your Feel-Good Hit Parade, will be featured next month. Every Wednesday dinner special is roast beef and mash, and every Friday is half-price cocktail hour in the lounge, featuring the piano tinklings of Ford Masters, fresh from his engagement at the Elks in Atherly.

So you've got a performance booked at the Big Chief Lodge, where you'll be playing three 45s per night. Whelan's father knew a guy who knew a guy who knew a guy enough of a price to pay to teach his son and his son's friend that the ropes were rough and made to bruise, and that if logic prevailed, they'd realize once and for all that music belonged in a church or maybe an opera house in continental Europe, which Orillia wasn't and didn't have. Whelan's father, on the other hand, hadn't thought of how happy you'd both be leaving the house in the late afternoon with your guitar cases, knowing you weren't heading to choir practice or music class, but to work.

You renamed yourself the Two-Timers. You sang songs by the Everly Brothers and Harry Belafonte.

"So, Silas, what do you think The Chief's next move will be?"

"From the icebox to the refrigerator, I figure!"

"I've heard that he wants to strengthen diplomatic ties with China."

"Well, you know The Chief: anything for a dish of egg chow mein!"

The ventriloquist might then have entered the little dressing room where you and Whelan were standing. If your first real adult musical experience was anything like mine, you'd be grinning, so happy and free to be on this perfect little piece of musical property, no matter how dank, small, or shitty it was in comparison to other places you'd come to know. The room appeared basic, yet it was yours; a refuge of solitude away from the hotel's noise and bustle. The ventriloquist threw his puppet on the ancient backstage couch, as if cleaning his palm of unwanted filth. The puppet lay there waving her arms like a drunken starlet. Sully tugged up his slacks, pulled a flask from his blazer pocket, ignited a Sweet Cap, downed the flask in one draw, and snarled, "Goddamned victims." Sure, the other half is aware, but they are powerless to stop themselves."

Although putting words in a made-up ventriloquist's mouth is one thing, Gord, putting words in yours and Whelan's is another thing. So try to not get mad at me for writing:

"Name's Whelan. This here's my friend, Gordon," your pal might have said, extending his hand.

"No offense, but I give a shit as much as that box of matches over there," said Sully, shooting his arm in the direction of the puppet.

"Gordon and I are playing here tonight. It's our first real gig," said Whelan.

"Well, in that case, know three things," said Sully. "One, the waitress with the big charlies has the clap. I should know because she got it from me. Two: don't trust the owner; he'll screw you eight ways to Sunday. And three: the cook horks in the chowder. Never order the chowder."

"Heck, we don't even like chowder," joked Whelan.

"What's the matter with this one?" asked Sully, pointing at you. "Doesn't this one talk?"

"No, I'll talk," you might have assured him.

"Apparently."

"We're all pretty new to this," said Whelan. "And if I might say, we're pretty darned excited."

Sully picked Silas up from the couch like a washerwoman grabbing a laundry rag. He drew a silk-lined box from under the couch and stuffed Silas in headfirst. Fighting the smoke that gathered about his eyes, Sully pinched the cigarette from between his teeth, exhaled with a grimace, then turned towards you and your friend.

"Well, you're not new anymore."

You and Whelan went out there and played. For me, Gord, my first gig was a thrilling and remarkable blur – a moment of glorious, if uncertain, fragments – and I wonder if yours was the same. After your set, you might have thought that people had listened to the songs, but you weren't sure. They'd eaten their food and applauded politely after every tune. Backstage, one of the waiters, a brush-cut kid who I'll call James – he had a quick smile and ears like New England clams – came and asked what kind of reward you were after. Not understanding, you stared at him until he said, "Beer or whiskey. But not wine. You're not going to be like that, are you?"

"Either would be great," said Whelan, answering for both of you.

"Great. Beers and a bottle of C.C. for my newest favorite performers," he said. "I get off at ten. Meet me at the dock. No one will be out. The temperature drops below 70 and the victims hit the sheets faster than your uncle on Jane Wyman," he said.

A while later, you left the Manitou and walked out the back of the hotel to the end of a long wooden dock, where James was lying on his back looking up at the sky, which had melted purple, speckled with stars.

"You did a lot better than most of them," he said, sitting up to *pfft* open three bottles of cold Pale Ale and pass them around. "Not a single complaint, which is pretty much how we measure things around here."

"People complain?" asked Whelan.

"Usually if it's too loud or if the musicians talk too much to the audience. Management doesn't want you to be much more than background music. You know, easy money and everything. Besides, those victims; all they want to do is eat their dinner and get back to fucking like monkeys."

"Sounds cool to me," said Whelan.

"Well, most of the performers who come through here learn how to cope, if you know what I mean," said James, drawing the twenty-sixer of C.C. from his bag and unscrewing the top.

"Sully doesn't seem to be coping so well," said Whelan. "That guy is some kind of weird."

"Still, he's a professional," he said, tugging on the whiskey and passing it around. "That's all management asks for. He does his show. He doesn't bother anyone. He's quiet. Although I'd like to turn that cornball dummy into firewood, given half the chance."

"Looks like Sully would do the same thing if it wasn't his meal ticket."

"Some meal. When he isn't working, the guy lives in his car. Never married. But he plays regularly. That's all you can really hope for in this racket," said James.

"Seems kind of lame. Just wanting that," you said, speaking for the first time.

"Marcel Marceau has an opinion?" said James.

"Yeah. Sometimes," you said.

"Hey, a shtick is a shtick. I've seen lots of acts come through here. And what you guys need is a shtick. Ever think of incorporating comedy into your act?"

"No," said Whelan. "You think that would work in a hit parade kind of show?"

"It might, it might," said James, taking a pull from his beer. "Don't really think it's been done before."

"Songs about this town. That hasn't been done before, either, you know," you said, realizing while you said it that the idea of a rock and roll song about Orillia and the land was pretty absurd. At the time, rock and roll was all about cars, girls, spaceships, crazy new dances, and haircuts. The trees and the animals be damned.

"This town?" said James. "Why the hell would anyone want to write about this town?"

"I don't know," you said, retreating into your thoughts.

"This town," spat James. "We're stuck to it like flies to a gluestrip. Just hanging there, limb by limb."

"You can always write about the gluestrip," you said, knowing that, really, you could not.

You lay on your back, swigging beer first, then whiskey (Collins says in his book that it was during these jobs that you developed a taste for alcohol). You considered what Sully was doing right now: sitting in the near-dark of his room while the TV painted his face in a brilliant patchwork of whatever scumbag show was shining through the glass. You considered what it meant to become what he'd become, and how you refused to be that not because of the loneliness and emptiness of the migrant entertainer's existence, but because you couldn't live with yourself if you didn't follow your gut instinct. What would it mean if you didn't write about how the forest darkened as the sun set as you followed your father along a scrub path after a day of fishing, walking back to the cottage where your uncles sat on lawn chairs drinking from mason jars with the kitchen light glowing behind them and the sound of women chirping inside while a baseball game barked on the transistor? You were so engrossed in this reminiscence that you didn't spot James pulling a tobacco pouch from his pocket, slivering a cigarette paper from his pocket, and tapping a thread of crumbled green leaf across the crease.

"Are you guys into marijuana?"

You were about to tell him that, no, you were new to it all: to the sensation of being alone playing music, to pot and booze, to people like Sully and James, to the idea of writing about the gluestrip, and to the possibilities that had once slept quietly in your dreams but now seemed to come to life. However, you did not. Because the puppeteer was correct: you were no longer new.

THURSDAY, JULY 13TH

Buddy Smith, the fugitive pitcher, was starving. He ate bugs and chewed hay. After that, he met Teresa Miller. He'd been lurking behind the barn, shoeless and dressed in his jail uniform. Mosquitoes had slashed his arms, legs, and neck as he walked through the bush before arriving at the farmhouse. He was cowering, hands balled into fists, preparing to pounce on whatever was approaching when he first heard the footfall. His eye teeth were loose in his head. Smith imagined himself in Paul Miller throwing a striped ball against the side of his boyhood home in Petrolia, pretending to be Whitey Ford, Bob Lemon, or Early Wynn. Besides, the child appeared astonished rather than afraid. He summoned his friend Gerard, and the two of them looked at the thirty-two-year-old escaped criminal as though a new playmate had arrived.

Buddy arose from the thick grass on the barn's side. He outran the kids and arrived at the house first. ""He was very polite,"Teresa Miller recounts. He mentioned being hungry, so I cooked him some sandwiches." Smith ate four of them - bologna and mustard - before Miller presented him with a massive slice of lemon meringue pie. The fugitive pitcher ate the dessert while Miller told him about the obstacles, the manhunt, and the 150 troops dispatched from Ottawa. Smith, sated, fatigued, and filthy, gazed around the kitchen, breathed in its aroma and warmth, and determined the woman was correct. Mrs. Miller dialed 911 and then handed the phone to the runaway pitcher. iller phoned the police, then passed the receiver to the fugitive pitcher. "He asked the police to give him enough time to finish eating his lunch and have a shave (before they came to get him)," she said. Smith noted that the youngsters had immediately realized that their visitor was one of the men who had escaped from a neighboring prison, at which moment the pitcher advised them not to be afraid. He wouldn't hurt them, and besides, he had his own sisters and mother. He sat at the table for a moment, his arms behind his back and resting in his chair. As it tipped back, the legs creaked. It was a pleasant sound.

The hall's attendants swept the game's ivory board clean with small, dark brushes; ceiling lamps were dimmed just so; and a handful of Russian officials stood whispering in their charge's ear as they cleared the television cameras from the room, found ice cubes for Bobby Fischer's orange juice, and covered the International Chess Federation's seal so that the American would no longer be distracted, hounded, persecuted, or whatever it was he claimed to be. Fischer's one-hour time limit expired, resulting in a forfeit and a 2-0 lead for Spassky. Privately, the Sovietskies cheered, and there was a sense that the American player, like the United States of America and capitalism itself, would consume itself, as everything with too many options and not enough discipline, doctrine, or direction would. "It was as if Fischer, were he a baseball player, had decided to go straight to the bottom of the ninth inning with the Russian ahead 5-0," one analyst explained. In the best of situations, coming back from a two-game deficit to win is difficult. It's very impossible to come back from a two-game deficit and win against a master like Spassky." And since everything about chess seemed to be everything that Fischer did not appear to be - lacking the composed and mechanical comportment required to play, as well as the stillness of thought required to shuffle through the permutations of infinite moves - the expert could have added that he was down two outs and hitting with a full count. It was raining; no, it was snowing; no, it was hailing. He was a strange figure standing alone at home plate.

Melvin Fisher was also alone. While incarcerated, he learned that transportation officials were meeting to consider civil liberties and privacy regulations, as well as the comfort of its passengers, in light of the recent hijacking plague. Melvin Fisher would be imprisoned indefinitely.

David McTaggart saw them coming: huge gray arrows piercing the ocean. The sounds was horrifying: huge machines gnashing their teeth, engines roaring beneath the ocean, beneath the globe. McTaggart waved his white flag, which must have appeared ridiculous to the French minesweepers. They arrived faster, their massive hulls thwoam thwoam as they hit the sea. One of McTaggart's new crew members yelled into his radio, "Stop Or You'll Face The Consequences Of The World's Court!" McTaggart, on the other hand, was unconcerned. Either the Vega would hold its ground, or he'd be swimming in the South Pacific in his heavy wet garments. It was unavoidable. It had to happen. It would be the first step toward making everything right, despite the lunacy and horror.

Colin Linden and his brother, Jay, went bowling at the Golden Mile Plaza on Thursday. "I was thinking ahead to Mariposa and what I could say in between songs," Colin recalled. 'When I left New York two years ago, I was ten. Now I'm sixty-two. I grew fifty-two years in two years and if that ain't the blues, tell me what is.' I repeated it over and over to myself all the time. I knew I'd use it. I had a plan."

stevie couldn't figure out the stones but who could and even if you could would you really want to know what lay at the heart of this thing that spat in the face of fame and calm and rock and roll bliss and almost single handedly tore apart whatever remained of sixties cool and tie-dyed togetherness or as jack batten reviewing the cobo hall show said, "detroit trembled in anticipation of terrible things, just as every city was supposed to." One of the Stones told a writer that Stevie and his boys couldn't jam or party, but was it really that necessary as long as the shows were terrific every night? But there was a catch: Stevie was good, but were the Stones? It all depends on who you ask. Some say they were a hot band molten to the core, while others say Richards especially played like shit warmed-over and jagger tried to put it on his back but he couldn't and besides there was jealousy because stevie was a few months away from putting out talking book with the song superstition which he gave to jeff beck but beck fucked with it so stevie took it back and when his friends found out I suppose he did, but even if Exile on Main Street has some fantastic songs on it, was it any more or less amazing than other bands' CDs that year? seventy-two gave us let's stay together by al green and neil's harvest and pink moon by nick drake and aretha's young gifted and black and something/anything by todd and, shit, pink floyd debuted dark side of the moon in january and ry cooder released into the purple valley and deep purple did machine head and big star had a number one record and randy newman came out with sail away and little feat – little feat! – had sailin' shoes and june gave us ziggy stardust roxy music lou reed and school's out by the coop and the harder they come and t rex's the slider and son of schmilsson and the band's rock of ages and backstabbers and all the young dudes by mott and even close to the edge by yes and a month later there was heavy cream and clear spot by captain beefheart and can't buy a thrill and another al green album called i'm still in love with you and in november neil followed up harvest with journey through the past and marlo thomas put out a kid's record that everyone owned called free to be ... both of us And the year finished with Marvin Gaye's Trouble Man and Lou Reed's Transformer because he shat songs faster than anyone could record them back then. So here were the Stones, surviving Detroit despite cops wielding ax-handled clubs, aerosol cans, and pistols, and while their tour was the biggest and most unruly in rock and roll history, it was crowded at the top man: shit they weren't even the biggest deal that weekend in a protestant backwater like Toronto, Ontario, can you believe it?

On Thursday, NDP leader David Lewis questioned External Affairs Minister Mitchell Sharp about "whether the government has been officially or in any other way informed by the government of France regarding the alleged ramming of Greenpeace III by a French minesweeper." Sharp answered, "I asked our embassy in France to get in touch with the French government because we had no information previously about the incident ... There are conflicting reports about the collision. The French ... said essentially that the two ships were passing slowly alongside each other, the French ship about to pass a message to Greenpeace. The Greenpeace turned by mistake, or was blown into the French ship. Damage was light, but the Greenpeace asked for help and was towed to Mururoa and repaired free of charge. The crew was hospitably treated."

Bobby Hull was the quarter-pounder of hockey, with his hairy arms and muscle-jawed jaw. Rod Laver in white shorts, Chianti wine in wicker globes, flower-patched bell-bottom jeans with a burlap belt, Elton John's sunglasses, Philly Soul, Jimmy Page's double neck and John Bonham's gong, mood rings, trucking songs, George Romero's films, Freddie Mercury's crotch pack Let It Be Dicey or Let It Be Nothing, Ali vs. Frazier, Lolas, velvet bullfighter paintings, Jonathan Livingston Seagull, Battle of the Network Stars, songs describing what it was like to be a native Indian by performers who weren't native Indians, Sid and Marty Krofft, Happiness is..., sad Cat Stevens song, Sweathogs, Trilogy of Terror "Seven Words You Can Never Say on Television," unisex aerosol, Jumpsuit chest hair, "Disco Duck," Avis vs. Hertz Eddie's Father's Courtship, "Jive Talkin'," OPEC, Lance Kerwin, Hot Wheels, Sanka, Bottle Caps, Quisp, Dynamints, Lik-A-Stix, and "Sit on it!," penny bags and tube tops, PCP, ELP, and GRT, strip malls, cigarettes, and gifts, The Beatles' death, Morton Shulman, Don Kirshner, Blaxploitation, sniffing PAM, Love's Baby Soft shampoo, Creepy Crawlers, "Wango Tango," Going Down the Road, Rick Azar and Commander Tom and Ed Shaunessy on the drums, Ancient qaps, Dr. Pepper, "Adriaaaaannnnn!!!", Fruit of the Loom, Chariot of the Gods.

On Thursday, Jim Slotek gathered everything he needed to fly to Toronto, which wasn't much because he was a teenager. His parents were worried because flights were being hijacked on a daily basis, but he really wanted to travel, and his brother would be there to show him around. He was fourteen years old and madly in love with rock & roll.

Jim's first trip to Mariposa '72 was to Toronto."I went with my brother, who was ten years older. It wasn't the sixties, but there were elements of hippie culture and all of that, being pre-disco, which would happen shortly thereafter. Walking around looking at everyone at the festival, it felt, to me, like the whole scene had fallen out of the sky. At one point, some lady started running around, shouting, 'Joe Cocker's here! Joe Cocker's here!' And it caused a commotion, for whatever reason. I remember seeing Lightfoot play. This was a big deal, at least to me; I knew all of his songs on guitar; most people did at the time. At one point, he sat down on a rock and started playing. A small crowd gathered around him."

Jim arrived in Toronto at a time when sceneries, motions, and noises were simultaneously dying and birthing. The year 1972 marked the beginning and end of a distinct era in Canadian music and culture. It marked the end of the songwriters scene in Yorkville and the beginning of the rock band period on Yonge Street. It was the end of colonial media and the beginning of Canada-centric TV shows - The Trouble with Tracy, The King of Kensington, and The Beachcombers, which debuted in September 1972 - as well as two new important networks: Global television and Citytv, both of which launched in 1972 and whose stock-in-trade was raw, shocking television (HBO launched that same summer in the United States).

The changes in Canada, and particularly in Toronto, were spurred by external factors as much as they were self-initiated. Gale Zoe Garnett, a singer/actor/writer who had already lived several lives as a pop star by 1972, claimed that Toronto's kinship with New York had a direct impact on local culture, even going so far as to point to a single event that, she claimed, helped move one city closer to the other and one decade out of the next. "From my perspective, everything changed after Bette Midler played the Continental Baths in New York City," she explained. "Afterwards, art and society and popular culture became very different from what they'd been before. At the Baths, there was always red liquid in the water cooler. Guys were running around with their towels tied on different sides to signify what they were or weren't into, and I grabbed one of them and pointed to the red liquid and I asked: 'Campari?' He replied: 'No, Lavoris [a mouthwash].' It was one of my favorite moments."

Midler, according to Garnett, introduced the heterosexual world to the homosexual world by crossing into the emerging gay culture of early 1970s New York, pushing music and art on a new, unknown road. "You could see the effect in Canada because there was such a large exchange between New York and Toronto." People would go down there, experience new things, and bring them back up north, ushering in the end of the 1960s. The sixties were an extremely hot era. It wasn't homophobic, but its physical appearance and design were, as was the musical culture, whether acoustic or electric. The whole disco phenomenon, which originated in France, became gayified, which opened things up. Reno Sweeneys was a restaurant in New York. I once opened for the singer Peter Allen there. I performed various songs as well as a few comedic or serious sequences. After my show, someone came backstage to tell me that Eric Bentley, a theater critic and translator, and Julie Christie were in the crowd and wanted to meet me. Lou Reed was sitting at their table when I went out to see them. I told him how much I admired his music and how much I admired him. He examined me and asked, 'Oh yeah? 'Would you like to suck my cock?' I said the first thing that came to mind: 'I dunno? "Can it sing?"

Garnett is adamant that the end of the 1960s and the beginning of the 1970s saw a shift in recreational drug use, with pot's rainbow softness giving way to coke's harsher edge. "It all started with the Hell's Angels at Altamont in 1969." I'd heard they did coke in addition to selling it. Coke didn't become popular until roughly 1972, and it transformed the mood of things. The problem with coke is that it's so high. The immortality begins as soon as the power begins. I didn't do a lot of coke - it's hard to write Shakespeare with your nose running - but, one time, I was driving along Bloor Street in Toronto and I heard myself exclaim, 'That's one pretty awful building. They should blow up the jerk.' I came to a halt somewhere between feeling fantastic and understanding I was turning into a power-tripping asshole with nose and tooth issues. If the sixties were all about the all-encompassing mellow that cannabis delivered, then coke came along and shattered it to bits with a massive hammer. The atmosphere of the times had changed dramatically."

In the summer of 1972, I purchased my first LP. While I don't know the exact date of the album's release - nor, apparently, does the Internet - my narrative impulses want it to be deep summer, say the second week of July, and just as the stars are appearing on the island, or the Stones are climbing the stage at Maple Leaf Gardens, or Pioneer 10 is tickling the asteroid belt, I'm handing over three dollars and ninety-nine cents of my parents' money before carrying the record under my arm to the family car The album catapulted me into a world of happiness, and decades later, I found myself creating songs and fronting my own band. Even though that was what I desired most in the summer of 1972, I had no idea it would ever happen.

Believe in Music was K-Tel's sun-drenched compilation. Its cover featured orange, red, and pink light streaks spreading from the top right corner of the jacket over a photo of a festival throng, with large seventies font stating the record's name as well as "22 Original Hits/Original Stars." The album began with "Brandy" by Looking Glass, a New Jersey band that would change their name twice, from Fallen Angels to Starz, before separating for good two years later, and ended with Gallery's "I Believe in Music," the compilation record's eponymous title cut. Songs by The Raspberries ("Go All the Way"), Donny Osmond ("Go Away Little Girl"), Dr. Hook ("Sylvia's Mother"), and Argent ("Hold Your Head Up") were interspersed. I listened to both sides with my parents sitting across from me on the couch the first time I ripped off the shrink wrap and played it on our light wood-grained basement's eight-track, turntable, cassette deck, and radio monolith. I recall how happy they were that I was happy, and how, in the end, the album wasn't a truncheon or a knife that divided us. Instead, we nodded along to tunes like "Let Your Yeah Be Yeah" by Brownsville Station, even though The Raspberries' teenage sex ballad made me feel strange. Still, for these reasons, rock and roll has always been more about getting along for me than blatant defiance.

Small record stores are rare nowadays, but they were common in my youth's new suburban landscape. I went to Music World in Albion Mall, A&A's in Sherway Gardens, Sam the Record Man in Royal York Plaza, and Sunrise music in Cloverdale Mall to buy music. Half of these stores were located in strip malls, between bowling lanes and Laura Secord chocolate shops.

Music was not exclusively sold in proper record stores in the 1970s. Sal's IGA had an album rack where US and People magazines are now sold. All of the hardware stores also sold LPs, as did Becker's Milk, a variety store that was supplied by label jobbers and independent distributors. I'd go to the plaza with my mom, and while she went shopping - drugstore, shoe repair, bakery, dry cleaner, supermarket - I'd hang out in Becker's, drinking chocolate milk and flipping through the latest Alice Cooper or Flying Burrito Brothers CD. It was at that store that I first heard of musicians like Laura Nyro and the Pure Prairie League. By the time we got home, I'd ripped off the shrink wrap and tossed the vinyl onto the turntable that my parents had permitted me to set up in my room.

Aside from the neighborhood strip mall depots, there were two Toronto record stores that every child in the 1970s knew about and tried to visit at least once a week: Sam the Record Man and A&A's on Yonge Street. It was like going to Maple Leaf Gardens, the CN Tower, or City Hall for me. They were vinyl temples, with a huge cardboard fresco of album covers patterning across the walls. Both businesses have three floors full of new and used releases.

I obtained a job working in a record store in 1979. It had always been a dream of mine. I was sixteen years old and working as a summer employee at Music World in the Albion Mall, a job that my father, a shopping mall builder, had assisted me in obtaining. The job was fine at first, almost dream-like. I was able to hang McCartney. Back to the Egg posters adorn the walls, "California Jam" T-shirts hang on the swag rack, and we test promo records provided to us by publicists every Tuesday, including albums by Emigre, Flash in the Pan, and The Monks. Because punk music had yet to make an impact in Etobicoke, the closest we came to replicating the record shop in Nick Hornby's High Fidelity was daring to play Bop till You Drop by Ry Cooder, Carolyne Mas, Damn the Torpedoes, or, if no one was looking, Look Sharp by Joe Jackson. Every morning, my supervisor, Frances, played Dylan's At Budokan (she also played it after lunch and twice in the evening). Back then, I couldn't grasp Dylan, partially because Cheap Trick had issued a song called Live at Budokan, which I adored. It disturbed me that someone regarded as a genius couldn't come up with a more creative name for his CD. I suggested to Frances one afternoon that we should play the two tracks back to back to demonstrate how superior I believed Cheap Trick's LP was. Frances shook her head, lit another du Maurier, and informed me, uh, no, we weren't going to do that. Then mom told me to take down the J. Geils Band poster and replaced it with a Billy Joel poster for Glass Houses, which I thought was a harsh punishment.

I wanted to steal the Back to the Egg poster, too, but it was too big. Things got worse for me after they hired a person to work evenings, and to watch over me during my afternoon shifts. She was a fifty something Scottish woman who hated music, and hated me more. Her actual job was to make sure I didn't give away too much change or allow shoplifters to shoplift too easily, but her unofficial job was to make sure that I got fired so that her nephew could work there. Having to deal with my sour workmate didn't help, but, in the end, I blew the gig on my own. I was fired just before the summer ended. They told me that I didn't have what it took, and that the old lady's nephew would be taking over my job. I asked if I could have the Joe Jackson poster that hung in the office. Frances said that I could. I went back there and folded Back to the Egg into the Look Sharp poster, and put them on my wall in our basement in Etobicoke, where, each time I looked at them, I was reminded that the world of selling stuff was no world for me. Soon it would be 1980, and, in October, the Rheostatics did their first gig. The seventies were over.

LETTER IN WHICH I CALL YOU A SELL-OUT (EVEN THOUGH YOU ARE NOT)

So Gord, you gave in. You sold out. You fell prey to what you vowed you'd never be. I'm kidding, actually. I'm kidding, but it's true that what you did in 1957 was something no one ever thought you'd do: you wrote a rock and roll song, or at least a novelty rock and roll song, about Hula Hoops.

Collins says that it's the first song you ever wrote, but I find that hard to believe (still, remember, you won't talk to me, so I don't know for sure). Anyway, you borrowed your dad's car and you headed back to Toronto, where you met Harold Moon, a publisher at BMI. Moon was a good guy, and he treated you with respect, even though you were only seventeen. I imagine that drive into town being the kind that most hopeful and budding artists take, believing that on the other end of the journey lies the great first payoff, the initial validation, the moment when you suddenly break through the thing that you've been butting against for most of your life. In the end, Moon didn't want the song, but it was okay. He looked at you across his big publishing-executive desk filled with papers and pens and stacks of sheet music and certificates framed on the wall behind him and he told you something that was almost as good as a publishing deal. He told you not to give up.

So you didn't. Instead, in 1958, you decided to go to Los Angeles, to the Westlake School of Modern Music. You liked jazz and had started playing drums with the Charlie Andrews Orchestra in Orillia. You read Downbeat – no, you devoured Downbeat – you and your pal Buddy Hill. At Westlake, you studied piano, orchestration, and musical theory. Lenny Soloman, the fiddler and violinist, told me: "Gordon has a real musicality. I did a session with him in 1974 or '75, and I got called to play some fiddle. It was a real eye-opener because he was so musically intelligent, not in the way I expected from a folk singer. He knew the chords, the flat five, all of the time signatures. He didn't need someone to translate his ideas for him. He was a musician first, and anyone not involved with him at that level couldn't have appreciated his knowledge."

Another story, from comic Harry Doupe, who met you at the Junos in 1996: "I was writing for the show. Aside from the Hall of Fame inductees, the only nod to the past was Gord singing 'If You Could Read My Mind.' I was at rehearsal at Copps Coliseum in Hamilton, and I was sitting at the front. They started up the tune, Gord began singing and he was horrible. His voice was just ridiculously bad. They ran through the song; reset, did it a few more times. After the song finished, he said, 'I saved the best one for last because Annie's here.' "

Doug McClement recalls working with you in Reno, Nevada, back in the 1990s. He was using his mobile studio van to record sound for a TV special. "Lightfoot has a system that has worked for decades, and he's neurotic about changing anything. When we did the show in Reno, the set designers asked if they could change the carpet that is used on stage under the band. Gord said no. When the keyboard player asked if he could move a keyboard onto a different stand to make it easier to play one of the songs, Gord said no. When the sound department wanted to swap out the mic on the acoustic guitar for a smaller one, Gord said no. He was just very meticulous and very much in control of his entire presentation. When Bob Doidge did the final mix at Grant Avenue Studios in

Hamilton, Gordon came in, spent a lot of time setting the volume levels on each track, then instructed Bob not to touch anything during the mix. So, like a good jazz group, the dynamics were all controlled by the musicians themselves. No fader moves."

Okay, then: Los Angeles. It was as strange back then as it has always been. It was undoubtedly stranger for you because you'd never lived somewhere else than Orillia. You departed Los Angeles after two years. It occurs. Many of my pals have also moved to Los Angeles. And New York; Canadians looking south for something bigger. It's difficult not to reach out and grab anything you can since a little bit of America can go a long way.

You probably never met her, Gord, because you were usually with music students, but have you heard of the songwriter Sharon Sheeley? Ken Tobias, a friend of mine, met her when he relocated to California in the 1960s to work for Bert Sugarman's publishing business. I realize this is your book, Gord, but I hope you don't mind if I tell you a story about Ken. You could even enjoy it. If it makes any difference, it's a California story via Canada.

Ken met Sharon while meditating by a little fountain at an ancient Hollywood monastery turned into an apartment/loft house. Ken may despise me for stating this, but I'm pretty sure he had a sleek, Greek Island Jesus-beard at the time, wore bell-bottoms with hippie wristbands, and probably wore a mood stone around his neck. Sharon, on the other hand, was dressed casually but elegantly. She was a slim woman with long black hair. When Ken initially went to Bert Sugarman's office, he ran into Mac Davis, who informed him that he thought Elvis might do one of his songs, either "Memories" or "In the Ghetto" or both. Anyway, Ken didn't have much luck, but he did meet Sharon Sheeley. In some ways, it was even lucky or better than selling a song to Elvis.

They decided to drive to the next gig one night after a show. The driver was young and arrogant, and he drove fast to please his heroes. When authorities combed through the wreckage, they discovered Eddie Cochran dead with his arm over his guitar case. Sharon and Gene were admitted to the hospital. Fans sent Sharon flowers, and telegrams from all over the world flooded in. She showed Ken images of herself in her hospital bed from old Photoplay magazines.

Ken never had a romantic relationship with Sharon, but he adored her. She assisted him in getting through California, specifically Los Angeles, while dealing with the worry that comes with being a musician attempting to make it in the United States. Sharon was well-versed in the local music scene. She eventually earned the acclaim she deserved and received awards for her songwriting. Don and Phil Everly, Ken's heroes, were introduced to him by Sharon. Don arrived in a vintage Cadillac to pick him up one evening, but Ken was shaking in the back seat. "Do not approach these guys as a fan. They think of you as a fellow musician, so straighten up. Straighten up, they think of you as a fellow musician."Eventually, Ken returned to Canada and lost touch with Sharon. I don't know if you consider yourself lucky, Gord, and I'm not suggesting that you are. All I'm saying is that sometimes people don't get the break they deserve, and sometimes people die without knowing how great they were. But I'm probably telling you something you already know and feel stupid for saying it.

FRIDAY, JULY 14TH

The Mariposa Folk Festival kicked up on Friday morning. Thousands gathered on the mainland's ferry terminal's cement dock before crossing through its tall white gates and down a small metal slope to the vessels. It was an old sound: feet stamping on the massive wooden deck while a cacophony of voices echoed out throughout the ship. As the foghorn blared and the boat began to move, people jammed buoy to buoy, engines growling as the hull slammed against the waves, showering those who stood along the railing. The sky was gray, and it was raining - lightly at first, then heavier as the day progressed - but it didn't matter. The ship lowered its gangway as it approached the island dock, and the festival-goers exited bandana and sandaled, their pipes stuffed in rucksacks, dope hidden in socks, granola packaged, and fruit, beer, and other items chilled in Coleman coolers. Younger kids in Mott the Hoople top hats and striped pants wandered towards the festival site along the shore of the island's dark canals, while another, smaller group - drugged, wild-haired, and dizzy-eyed - ran from the dock in search of the strongest crook in the longest branch of the tallest tree, from which they would observe the entire festival, occasionally mewling and scrawling.

Volunteers standing inside the red snow-fence that separated the event from the rest of the island gave out newspaper programs. The cover of the program included an aboriginal depiction of a loon painted by Saul Williams, an eighteen-year-old Ojibway boy from Weagamow, Ontario, whose art would be gathered and shown at the Royal Ontario Museum two decades later. Adrienne Leban's illustration on the back cover was a full-color, pointillist portrayal of planets revolving around the sun, with a celestial ography of half moons, arrows, and 69 drawn at the top of the page. At the bottom, the date and time were scribbled in freehand: Toronto, Canada, July 14, 10:30 a.m. The rest of the program was filled with odd bits - an ad for Yorkdale Shopping Centre ("Canada's Fashion Centre"), TSS recording studio, BMI music, a local Gulf service station, the Brau Haus restaurant, and Stompin' Tom's label, Boot Records - but none was odder than a favorable two-page auditor's report from the 1971 festival, published on pages 25 and 26. There were also lengthy artist biographies and photographs of shawled women and sideburns men, as well as an odd essay titled "Videovision versus Television."

The crowd, which had grown to 14,000 by Saturday morning, had gathered in front of the six stages, with people laying down their blankets on the damp summer grass. Ken Whiteley, a member of the Original Sloth Band, had his first Mariposa appearance in 1972. "I've always said that I didn't go to university," he tells me, "I went to folk festivals. There was so much to learn and to absorb. In '72, I sat around playing with David Wilcox and Peter Ecklund, the trumpet player [Gregg Allman, Paul Butterfield], and we had this swing jam. Ted Bogan joined in and he taught me swing chords I never knew before. At a later festival, I remember playing with Dewey Balfa and listening to him say, 'Now, there are six different ways to accompany a Cajun waltz.' By the end of every Mariposa, I'd absorbed so much."

Gordon Flagler, a Crowbar fan from Ottawa, hitchhiked to the festival because "Mariposa '72 was one of the first gatherings of the tribes. Before '72, hippie culture was only in Toronto, but it had started to spread, and one of the things about that weekend was that everyone was coming together. You watch the movie, Festival Express, which was made in 1970, and pretty much everyone in the crowd has short hair. But the freaks were out in '72, and you could feel that on the island. The festival had the feeling of triumph for our culture. It was as if, after years of fighting against traditional ways and values and all of that, people just said, 'Fuck it,' and did whatever they wanted. I battled with my father about my beard and my hair and other things, but by 1972, I'd just worn him down. They got tired of fighting us."

The grounds ultimately got crowded with people like Flagler, festival-goers breaking beers, pouring wine into small glasses, and using dope and hash. Fans were buzzed and pancaked to the ground as they studied the festival's schedule, which was folioed in the middle of the program and inscribed in freehand on a grid in broad seventies script: 3 p.m. Roosevelt Sykes and Bonnie Raitt on Stage

One; 5 p.m. Bukka White on Stage Six; and 7 p.m. Taj Mahal on Stage Three. On Saturday, John Prine, dressed in blue denim jeans, shirt, and jacket, would host a tribute to Hank Williams; Murray McLauchlan and David Bromberg would play and discuss Bob Dylan's influences; Alice Seeger would lead a workshop called "The Oppression of Women in Song," and Bruce Cockburn would perform the late set on Sunday night. Cockburn had previously performed at the festival in 1971. That year, Estelle Klein requested him to guard the backstage "stockade" while the governing area coordinator was on vacation. At one time, James Taylor, a surprise guest in 1971, requested admission, but Bruce refused. "I just figured that rules were rules, and so I did what Estelle said." He was nice, but it was obvious that he wanted in. It was also evident that I wasn't going to let him. Finally, Lightfoot appeared and saved me. 'You know, Bruce, I really think it would be okay if you let James Taylor into the artists' tent,' he added.

Mariposa '72 included a mix of the well-known and the obscure, the tough and the simple. Bonnie Raitt, freckled and twenty-three years old in 1972, was on one end of the range, while Prine, a young American songwriter, was on the other. If they weren't already part of American musical history, they were surely at the forefront of the current sound. Prince had only recently emerged on the radar of music lovers, despite working as a mailman in Maywood, Illinois, barely eighteen months previously. After seeing him sing on open mic night at the Fifth Peg folk club, film critic Roger Ebert wrote the first review of his music. "After the rumor started to circulate that Dylan might be coming to the island," Bruce Cockburn says of Prine's Mariposa shows, "people heard Prine's voice coming from another stage, and went to it, thinking it was Bob singing."

Gordon Flagler, an Ottawa Crowbar enthusiast, hitchhiked to the festival because "Mariposa '72 was one of the first tribe gatherings." Before 1972, hippie culture was limited to Toronto, but it had begun to expand, and one of the highlights of that weekend was the fact that everyone was gathering together. When you watch the 1970 film Festival Express, almost everyone in the audience has short hair. But the freaks were out in '72, and it was palpable on the island. The celebration exuded a sense of success for our culture. It was as if, after years of fighting against established methods and beliefs, people finally yelled, 'Fuck it,' and did whatever they wanted. I fought with my father over my beard, hair, and other issues, but by 1972, I'd simply worn him down. They were sick of fighting us."

The grounds eventually became congested with festival-goers smashing beers, pouring wine into little glasses, and using dope and hash. The festival's schedule was folioed in the middle of the program and inscribed in freehand on a grid in broad seventies script: 3 p.m. Roosevelt Sykes and Bonnie Raitt on Stage One; 5 p.m. Bukka White on Stage Six; and 7 p.m. Taj Mahal on Stage Three. On Saturday, John Prine would host a tribute to Hank Williams, dressed in blue denim jeans, shirt, and jacket; Murray McLauchlan and David Bromberg would play and discuss Bob Dylan's influences; Alice Seeger would lead a workshop called "The Oppression of Women in Song," and Bruce Cockburn would perform the late set on Sunday night.

Mariposa '72 included a mix of well-known and obscure artists, as well as the tough and the simple. In 1972, Bonnie Raitt, freckled and twenty-three years old, was on one end of the spectrum, and John Prine, a young American songwriter, was on the other. They were at the forefront of the contemporary sound, if not already part of American musical history.

Kilby Snow was also present in Mariposa. Snow, dubbed "the Bill Monroe of the autoharp," learned the instrument at such a young age that he performed at dances, socials, and bars while still under the age of majority. The Wareham Brothers, from Harbour Buffet, a little island in the center of Placentia Bay in Newfoundland, felt the same way. They'd never actually had a proper gig before coming to Mariposa. Instead, it was largely house parties and dances, which ceased when the Smallwood government relocated Harbour Buffet to Arnold's Cove.

Honey Novick was tasked with looking after the old Inuit folk singers as well as John Prine."It was the first time any of them had been out of the North," she said, "so, one afternoon, I decided to bring them into the city. I took them on the subway, which terrified them. They found the trains so fast, and even though it was a moderate weekend, temperature-wise, the heat was stifling to them. They were astounded by the city, by Yonge Street. We didn't understand each other, but we communicated the same way I'd communicated with a very drunken John Prine: through facial expressions and the occasional silent hand gesture. It's hard to know for sure what the impact of the weekend was on the elders, but, for me, it was an experience that ended up changing the course of my life. Our worlds were unfolding in strange and different ways, and we were right there in the middle of it."

Because this book is set in the folk realm of the 1960s and 1970s, it was only a matter of time before it collided with someone named Skye, and so Skye Morrison appeared at Mariposa early Friday morning. It was her task, along with a few others, to get the craft area up and running; setting up the tables, rigging the kilns, and ensuring that all of the craftsmen were where they were supposed to be, which had been distributed all over town the night before.

"[My parents] were some of the original folkies," she explained to me. "When I was born, I was known as a 'red diaper baby,' being the child of left-leaning parents from Western Canada. Marian Anderson, the American opera singer, was taken to the Macdonald Hotel in Edmonton - the old CN hotel - when I was five years old, the first time a black person had ever been permitted in. They ate dinner, and it became a major news item. My parents took me to Mariposa when I was eight years old after we moved east, and it became a part of my cultural life. There were many explicitly political songs on the folk music scene, but it was also a populist means of presenting the world's reality. Even at such a young age, it was difficult not to learn something from them.

"Mariposa in '72 was still a lot more like what Newport would have been eight or ten years earlier. It maintained its integrity because of its devotion to traditional artists and to its ideology, which included craftspeople and artisans as well. It had an authenticity despite a changing world and changing music scenes, and those who ran it still believed that there could be a connection between music and people. Remember: the stages were one foot off the ground. Even though the musicians were held in very high regard and valued above all, they were presented on equal terms with the audience. Having gone to high school with Chris and Ken Whiteley, and known Joni Mitchell back when she was Joni Anderson, they were just people [to me]: extremely talented people. When they all returned to Mariposa in '72, it wasn't that big a deal because a lot of us thought, 'They came from here and here is where they're supposed to be.' "

Mariposa had endeavored from the beginning to place the craft area and the artisans on equal footing, but they were always considered as curiosities at a music festival. They performed on the outskirts of the festival grounds, despite the fact that many of them were as inventive as the musicians themselves.The native area and the craft section were close to each other, thus the presenters got along well.

Gordon Flagler recalls: "In between the headliners, my friends and I would watch all of the amazing traditional musicians; people like Jean Carignan, the legendary fiddler from Lévis, Quebec. He'd do workshops with Rufus Guinchard. They'd play a Quebecois tune, a Celtic tune, a Newfoundland tune, and then Jean would play something by Bob Wills, with whom he'd toured as a young man. It was incredible: all of this deep musical history coming alive right in front of you. It's not like it is today, when you can see traditional and folk musicians performing at most places at different times during the year. Back then, people wouldn't hire them to play normal clubs, and that's why Jean Carignan drove a cab. He couldn't make a living despite being an incredible musician. Mariposa was our one opportunity to see and hear them, and, in '72, you had these stars – these huge artists – hanging out and playing, as well."

While thousands of people gathered on the isthmus for the first day of Mariposa, police radios reported that Donald Oag was in Ottawa. They'd discovered a car there, a '53 Chevy Nova reported lost from Kingston on Wednesday morning. The prints of Oag were on the driving wheel, as were those of Thomas McCauley, who had been sighted on Bank Street. McCauley was the first prisoner to escape from Millhaven, months before the July jailbreak, and if authorities suspected the two men were working together, they also assumed Oag handled the heavy lifting while McCauley, the senior of the two, plotted how to proceed. Mr. Lalande died as a result of strangulation, according to an autopsy. Lalande was discovered naked on the floor near the bed. His wrists and feet were bound with a clothesline, and a rag was put into his mouth. Before fleeing into the night, one of the killers tore a sheet from Lalande's bed, letting it ripple in the air like a manta ray's wings, and draped it over the victim's body.

In France, Friday was Bastille Day. Thousands lined the Champs-Élysées to see the yearly procession. Flags were waved, champagne was consumed, and flowers were thrown. Vendors sold chestnuts, and cafes were packed. The introduction of a seventy-foot-long surface-to-surface missile with a range of approximately 3,000 kilometers, according to Reuters, was the event's high point. Its arrival, however, proved unlucky as the truck transporting the rocket broke down in front of the audience. Even so, the weapon seemed immense, especially since it was in the shadow of the Eiffel Tower. It was intended to carry a nuclear warhead weighing 150 kilograms, nearly twice the size of the last French bomb. Authorities stated that this one, too, needed to be tested. France would be the world's nuclear powerhouse. They would demonstrate to the United States and Russia that, when it came to military might, this effete Gallic republic could compete with them on the world arena.

On Friday, Bobby Fischer must have shocked himself, though it's difficult to say for sure, because it was evident that he was "sumashedski," a term used by the park-bench players in Moscow to describe the American challenger's erratic behavior. Even though it had been nearly twenty-four hours since Fischer had sat across from Spassky and played, Fischer continued to press for additional demands. Fischer's most recent demand was the most unreasonable: he wanted to change rooms. He wanted the match to be held in a small table-tennis room at the back of the hall, away from prying eyes and the hot menace of the TV camera lens, which he claimed were damaging both his psyche and the summit's integrity.

It's difficult to imagine any player or athlete in any sport now having more control over their game than the TV networks, which now spend unfathomable billions for broadcasting rights. But that summer in Iceland, Fischer's bravado, boldness, cunning, and arrogance towered over the match and its organizers, who'd worked painstakingly to create it at a time when the United States and Russia were embroiled in a diplomatic standoff. The organizers relented. They took everything into the table-tennis room, where a single closed-circuit camera broadcasted footage to the hall audience. McTaggart repaired his ship, returned to the atoll, and was rammed again in 1974. He was thrashed much more severely. McTaggart, on the other hand, took photographs this time. The photographs were smuggled and leaked to the media. McTaggart filed a lawsuit against the French government, and there were marches: three or four in Paris that summer, asking that the government stop doing what it had been doing for years. When McTaggart's case was heard, the French court ruled against their own government in a landmark ruling. The nuclear program was brought to its knees. Finally, France stopped conducting atmospheric nuclear tests, and authorities promised to leave Mururoa alone. McTaggart halted to rejoice, but by the time the decision was delivered, he had moved on. Nuclear waste was contaminating the oceans. Mining and oil prospecting were wreaking havoc on Antarctica. And then there are the whales. The whales required assistance.

Garth Douglas and a friend traveled to Centre Island on Friday, arriving late at night. "When we got there," he explained, "we saw right away that Mariposa was sold out." We'd gone with the vague idea that something was going on and that we wanted to be a part of it." Douglas and his companion were both eighteen years old at the time. They were standing on the lagoon coast near Algonquin Island with around three thousand other people when they observed a rickety hurricane fence on the other side. It was a hot day, and the water seemed refreshing.

The press release was issued on Friday by Pravda. The names Kharlamov, Yakushev, Mikhailov, Petrov, Tretiak, Gusev, Blinov, Anisin, and others were announced in a two-inch column in the sports pages of the Globe and Mail. They had strange names that had nothing to do with hockey. They were enigmatic and odd, and no one could put a weight on them. Still, Harry Sinden felt compelled to speak up."These Russians are better than any other Russian team," he told the press. "No one has asked me for a prediction, so I'll say it anyway: This will be a good series."

Everyone else was breaking out of the prison that day, so he had no choice but to join them. While inside, he'd written letters home to his parents, describing the cacophony of sounds that woke him up every morning: a symphony of septum-clanging snoring; the predictable and weary shuffling of guards towards the cells; the morning clarion of the baton rattling across prison doors; the garbled protestations of formerly sleeping inmates and the guards swearing them awake; farting, creaking, y Once outside, Rudolph was propelled by his imagination rather than his legs, anxiety, or pulse rate. It got him further than any other inmate. The majority of the inmates had been transferred to neighboring counties, but Rudolph went above and above.

Police thought about looking for him at his home in Niagara-on-the-Lake, but it was preposterous to think that he could have made it that far, not with all of the roadblocks and provincial and federal authorities prowling the depths of the bush from Pickering to Sydenham. But they found no trace of Rudolph in the immediate area, and, for a moment, some wondered whether he'd been murdered by another inmate, but who would have had the time and what would they have done with the body?

On Friday, the government announced that, despite pressure from fans, it would not take the initiative to persuade NHL owners to let Bobby Hull play for Team Canada. Before long, Hockey Canada's Phil Reimer had resigned as governor of the organization and billboard magnate Claude Neon – a real shit disturber – announced he was putting up over 300 billboards across the country: TO HULL WITH RUSSIA (the signs were erected overnight). In Alberta, 23,000 people marched in the streets of Edmonton protesting the WHA player's absence; the long-hairs at CHUM radio in Toronto and CJAD in Montreal organized a series of listener petitions; and hundreds of others telephoned and sent letters to Munro's office, one of them accusing the NHL of "raping Canadian hockey."

All of this made Harry's head hurt. Sure, he wanted Bobby Hull on his team, but there were other things to worry about. Like Orr. Nobody wanted to talk about Orr: how he could barely skate on those goddamn knees; how it hurt when he stood up to piss. You think those WHA fly-by-nighters never waved a mill' or two or three or four in front of Orr's nose? Hull bit, and, because he bit, he'd created a goddamned mess that Harry didn't need.

There was something else nagging at Harry. It was a feeling he was loath to explain to his friends or associates lest it come out sounding like some sort of inarticulate lunacy. Besides, the nature of the series demanded that he remain square-shouldered and resolute in his determination and leadership. Any sense of doubt would be considered a weakness, and damned if he was going to give the Russians reasons to believe that they could penetrate the famous Canadian resolve.

Roberta Richards had to get Bukka White his medicine on Friday at Mariposa. This could refer to actual medicine, but it could also refer to something else. "On the Friday of most festivals, Bukka likes to tell people that it will be his forty-ninth birthday on Sunday," said Roberta, who now lives in Guelph, Ontario, with her family. "Of course, his birthday was celebrated at every festival. 'I'm not asking for gifts, you know, but if you want to bring me something, I enjoy bourbon,' he'd remark. There was enough wine by the conclusion of the festival to make an army drunk."
Estelle Klein had entrusted Roberta with the festival's blues concerts because she had promoted blues performers since she was sixteen years old. Roberta grew up "practically in a trunk." Her grandfathers were both theater promoters, one in Toronto and the other in New York City. Her grandparents in Toronto organized events with artists ranging from Jimmy Crawford to Duke Ellington, who frequently stayed at their Bathurst and College home due to discriminatory local hotel laws. This was my musical education, and when I returned to Toronto, the folk culture was

thriving in the Yorkville bars. I never truly grasped it. Many folks in Yorkville were writing songs about lost loves, their dog dying, and their truck breaking down, and I got the impression that they had a very strict agenda. They wrote depressing songs about how horrible everything could be, but I'd met rural blues people who knew how bad things could be. It wasn't horrible what these folk singers were singing about. There are some songs that are optimistic in the midst of loss or disaster, but a lot of folk music at the time just didn't get it."

Roberta began booking bands in Toronto, focusing on blues. "When I first met Bukka White, he told me his name was Booker T. Washington White but that I should call him 'Big Daddy,'" she explained. "Roosevelt Sykes was also very sweet. Roosevelt Sykes was very sweet, too. He was religious, and when the others would go off for their 'medicine,' he would just bow his head and say grace. The hospitality often left them wanting, too, so I'd take them out for dinner to the Underground Railroad [an old restaurant in Toronto named after the passageway by which American slaves fled to Canada] and they would dig in. They understood the significance of the restaurant's name. I sat there listening for hours as they talked about their families, telling stories of slavery."

Colin Linden, his mother, and his brother packed their bedrolls and blankets and drove to the lake on Friday. They were on their way to Mariposa. "I'd studied the program for every other Mariposa," he said. "I'd read all of the bios and advertisements; memorized the clubs, record labels, and radio stations." I saw an ad for Fiddler's Green and began hanging around there, seeing a number of musicians, many of whom were at the festival. When we arrived on the ferry, there were already a lot of people on board. My performance was on an open stage - stage three, to be precise - and it was the best day of my life up to that moment. It was my first time performing in front of an audience, and it opened my eyes to so many things. The morning began with a dulcimer session with Bruce Cockburn, but I recall seeing him sitting at a picnic table before that. I approached him and introduced myself; he recalls our meeting to this day.There were many connections created that day, both among everyone and among myself. Before my set, which was hosted by Chick Roberts, I was warming up on a small tree stump when a man approached and began talking to me. He was curious about who I was, where I was from, and what I was all about. He asked when I was going to play, and I told him, and he said he was going to come and watch. I didn't think much of it at the time, but when I peered out into the throng, there he was: John Prine, who'd just released his debut album. 'When I left New York City two years ago, I was ten years old,' I informed the audience. I'm now sixty-two years old, so I've grown fifty-two years in two years. If that's not the blues, I'm not sure what is.' Chick suggested that I play the next day after my set, but I didn't want to come across as greedy or anything. But he encouraged me, telling me that everything was all right. As a result, I did. John Allan Cameron, the legendary Cape Breton songwriter, emceed the event. After that, my brother and I went for a walk just as the sun began to set. That's when we ran into Lightfoot and the Goods, who were sitting at a picnic table, simply playing.

"The thing that was great about Mariposa was that it was an environment that was cool enough for all of those stars to be at, and to hang around, but it was also cool enough for a kid like me to play. For a second, those two realities coexisted, and it was rare and very special. There was a very clear connection being made between musicians at every level, whether you were a beginner, or whether you were signed to a label and had made hit records. Being on a small island helped all of that, of course, and being on a small island just off the shore of Toronto factored into whatever magic was at play. Some dyed-in-the-wool Mariposa-ites thought that having these stars ruined it for everybody, and that always sort of saddened me. There was something that was very self-defeating about that attitude, and, as a result, the next year Mariposa went out of its way to make sure that no one famous showed up, and really, that no one would have any fun. Still, the Winnipeg Folk Festival was hatched in '74 because of what Mariposa did. Same with Festival of Friends and Hamilton in '76, and the Home County Festival in London. They put festivals on the map in Canada. It was a true beginning for me, and for countless others."

LETTER IN WHICH I ASK YOU ABOUT DYLAN, AND IN WHICH I GO ON A TRIP UP NORTH

Gord, the good days arrived in 1965. Every vocalist aspires to erupt, and Gord, you did. Albert Grossman was your manager, and he landed you a record deal with United Artists. Many others covered your successful songs before anyone outside of Toronto even knew who you were. Marty Robbins ("Ribbon of Darkness"), George Hamilton IV ("Steel Rail Blues"), Peter, Paul and Mary, and Johnny Cash all covered you. How does it feel to be covered by Johnny Cash, Gord? It's kind of like being covered by Gordon Lightfoot, which has occurred previously. "I was at Massey Hall on May 6, 1998," says Harry Dupe. Gord was introducing a new song, 'by my friend, Steve, and I've heard it played a lot around the Muskoka bars,' he said. It's called "I Used to Be a Country Singer," and Gord performs it to a standing ovation. When he's finished, he glances down at the audience and sees Steve seated towards the front of the stage. 'Hey, good one, pal!' he says to Steve. I believe they enjoy it!'Then Gord turns to the audience and says, 'Jeez, I don't know how I'm going to follow that.' The band then begins playing "Wreck of the Edmund Fitzgerald."

People were going crazy over you pretty quickly. You won Folksinger of the Year, beating out Joni, Ian, and Sylvia, as well as that strange poet with the big schnozz, Montrealer Leonard Cohen. "Ribbon of Darkness" was chosen the finest country song of the year by the American Society of Composers, Authors, and Publishers. Your music captured the essence of the Canadian soul at a time when Canadians were still figuring out who they were and what they stood for. You provided your people a platform. You provided them with a musical hero. "There was a time in Canada when people would say, for instance, 'Well, Pierre Berton is a really bright guy, but he's no Norman Mailer,' or 'He'd get torn up if he debated William F. Buckley.' But in music, you couldn't say that about Lightfoot. You couldn't say, 'Well, he's good for a Canadian' because he was the first musician from here to be very highly regarded internationally. People don't realize the effect now, and it's hard, because there are tons of Canadian stars. But back then, there weren't, and to have him achieve at such a high level was very socially and culturally important."

People began referring to you as "Canada's Bob Dylan" - even "The New Dylan" - in 1967, but I'm not sure that impressed you (for the record, I've always thought of you as "Canada's Bob Marley," a person whose music translates wherever it's played while also retaining a very strong sense of place). The phrase "The New Dylan" has always been a bit of a curse, and it's a touch tired these days. Anyone who has ever sung a song through their septum about a one-eyed pirate making love to a peg-legged gypsy while someplace an unjust war is going on has been dubbed the "new Dylan." Anyone anyone shuffled along with their hands crammed in the pockets of their checkered bomber jacket while wearing a proletarian cap? Yes, Dylan is the new Dylan. And anyone who has ever written an elegy about injustice set to three chords and a bridge in either A minor, B minor, or D minor and named it after something they saw in whatever room they were sitting in - "Ballad of a Withered Potted Plant" or "Musings of a Budgie in a Wrought-Iron Cage" - then given that song a random number - "Tiger-Stripe Hoop Skirt #327"
Marcel Khalifé, a Lebanese folk singer, has been dubbed the "new Dylan." Carlos Verela of Cuba has done the same. Donovan Leitch was as well, but we all know how that worked out. Jean Ferrat, Steve Forbert, Bruce Springsteen, Loudon Wainwright III, Arlo Guthrie, and John Prine were all considered the new Dylan. Jakob, Bob's youngest son, has also been dubbed "the new Dylan." Biologically, this is correct.

Don Kerr, my bandmate and buddy, has accomplished a great deal. However, Bob Dylan addressed him on his radio show one evening, so you can shoot him now, though I wouldn't recommend it. Bruce McDonald, a filmmaker, has never met Bob Dylan, yet making a tale about him has made him all the more essential to those who judge the worth of others in such terms. Gina Gershon, the actress, is the one who wrote the narrative. Gina decided to take boxing lessons one summer in Los Angeles. She was having a great time and increasing her skills when her coach suggested that she spar with someone to test how far she'd progressed. This sounded fine to her, so she climbed into the ring the next day to discover a man of comparable weight and height warming up on the ropes. After the bell rang, she moved into the center of the ring, where Dylan, squished into his hat, appeared. Gina still hit him.

Dylan was dreadful in concert the one time I saw him. It occurs. No band, singer, or musician is immune to terrible performances. We were seated a few seats away from Hurricane Carter, upon whom Dylan penned the song "Hurricane," which helped win Carter's release from prison. Carter used to live just a few blocks from me in Toronto, and he kept his Christmas lights up all year. He wore a straw hat and wire-rimmed glasses and had massive calves. I never watered my walkway around him because he appeared like a kind guy. One neighbor who did was chastised by the old boxer, who had the kind of fury you'd expect from someone who used to strike people for a job.

Dylan's music was lost on me since I was a hardrock album rat in the mid-1970s. His best music was certainly behind him, and as a result, songs like Street Legal and Slow Train Coming were perplexing to me. Although these albums delighted my stoner cousins, who were old enough to remember his voice's first impression, I shrugged because they weren't Wings Over America, Ummagumma, or Houses of the Holy.

Dylan has performed numerous times in Toronto. He's been on the CBC, too, strolling with his guitar through a fake log-cabin set built by men from small towns in Europe who lived on Concord, Montrose, and Crawford Street, working-class neighborhood men who probably saw Dylan as some kind of braying, unbathed, over-sexed, and talentless urchin not fit to scrape your boot heel, Gord. To them, you were a man's man, your piney tenor conveying character, resolve, and an honest work ethic, whereas Dylan was a big-city phony who dressed up and sang in a language only stoned people could understand. But he wasn't you. Nobody was.
You were a fan of Bob Dylan's music. I know this because Al Mair informed me you're a ""110 percent Dylan fan." From a distance, it appears that the feeling is mutual, but as Cathy Evelyn Smith writes in her book - which you should probably not read - whenever you

guys hung out, the occasion was laden with anxiety and ambiguity. There's a story about you meeting Dylan before Newport, but it sounds like it came from the Church of Bob, so it can't be completely trusted. According to legend, Albert Grossman introduced you to him, and the two of you planned to hang out one night in New York City. Someone suggested you try your hand at the pool. Someone (likely Dylan) may have said:

-Hey, man, you any good at pool? Cause I am, and I need something to chew on.
Then someone else (probably you) might have said:
-Yeah, sure, pool. Sounds good.
-But you can play, right?
-Sure I can play.
-Whaddya shoot, Gord?
-Whaddya mean what do I shoot?
-You know, what's your handicap?
-Oh. Um. I dunno. Maybe an eight?
-An eight? Jeezus. Even Van Ronk's a six. You sure you're only an eight?
-Well, maybe a seven. On a good night.
-Well, Gord. Here's hoping you're right.

Maynard Collins' book reveals how poorly you played that night, how your shortcomings as a snookerist were exposed.
-That's no seven handicap, Gord! That's maybe a nine or ten at best!
You may not have cared that you lost to Dylan - losing to Dylan was something that artists of all levels did on a daily basis - but Collins claims that "after the game, Gord went on to become a very good pool player." So perhaps you did care. Perhaps Collins is channeling the Church of Bob. Maybe losing to Dylan was a disgrace you couldn't bear, and you still fantasize about beating Dylan, that arrogant little flop-headed bastard from northern Minnesota, in a rematch, before harpooning your cue through his stomach, as I type this.

Maybe you were fed into the jaws of the great artist, the highly-driven and competitive folk-rock superstar loving every moment, like Donovan in Don't Look Back. Perhaps he laughed when you missed a shot. Maybe he made fun of your clothes - your trousers, plaid shirt, and shoes - and then he made fun of your voice: -That shot was far "ooot," guy. It was significantly more "ooot!"

Or perhaps he was leaning against a plywood wall drenched in Rolling Rock neon, his arm around the waist of a fine-boned Vassarite slumming it in the trenches. Perhaps he laughed as you missed the pocket. Maybe you strolled over to your date, who, according to Grossman, should be a lower-rent Vassarite, a petit C-list actress like Selma Jean or something. Perhaps you missed the shot on purpose, battling your competitive instincts. Maybe you lost just to make your hero happy. Perhaps you were defeated because you are Canadian. Because you are a lovely person.

But I'm not sure.

You're not going to talk to me.

At this point, Gord, I should do something that biographies need. I should serve the interests of readers who will be interested in the banal details of your existence. For instance, some people will want to know that 1) you like to shower wearing latex gloves so your calluses won't soften (it's a weird image, thinking of you doing that); or 2) you like to collect CHUM Charts (I read that on the CHUM Chart site); or 3) you were asked to play at The Last Waltz, but you refused because "I didn't feel I had the confidence to do it," (Seattle Weekly) even though you were there at Winterland to say goodbye to The Band; or 4) your mother once told the press that, when you were a kid, you used to sing to yourself for an hour before you fell asleep; or 5) the songwriter, Phil Ochs, wrote his famous song, "Changes," while hanging out in your place on Admiral Street, where you lived with Brita; or 6) you annotate and construct all of your own songbooks; or 7) a famous actor who was sleeping with Cathy Smith used to belittle you by calling you "Footsie," and who once, after shagging Cathy in your hotel room, charged champagne and caviar in your name; or 8) you acted in a film called Harry Tracy, Desperado; or 9) you invested your money in apartments and plazas and now have over a gajillion dollars to your name; or 10) you record most of your song ideas on a cassette recorder, often while you're sitting around watching the Leafs play (you've done a lot of estimable things, Gord, but finding inspiration in the godawful Leafs might be your greatest achievement). All of these things are interesting, to be sure, but I'm not convinced they reveal anything about who you are or why I'm writing about you in the first place.

SATURDAY AND SUNDAY, JULY 15TH AND 16TH

The celebs who weren't supposed to come to Mariposa showed up on Saturday and Sunday. "Bob Dylan, rarely seen in the past five years, hugged Gordon Lightfoot before escaping from fans running after him," wrote Peter Goddard in the Toronto Star. As Joni Mitchell looked on, Neil Young led 4,000 people in a singing. The small figure of Dylan, dressed in pants, a white shirt, a red bandana, and rimless spectacles, was central to this. A passerby handed him a bottle of beer, and he circled the throng, briefly watching some ancient fiddlers before moving to another section to listen to Roosevelt Sykes and Bukka White. 'We were vacationing in the area, and decided to drop in,' he said. "We've been here for Mariposa's three days," he said. 'We even got rained out like everyone else on Saturday night.' "

The Saskatoon-born songwriter had released her seminal album, Blue, ten months previously, and on June 15, 1972, she delivered her final gig at the Olympia in Paris before returning to California. Much of the tour had been opened by Jackson Browne, and the two musicians had been intimately linked (Honey Novick recounted riding the ferry with them and how "they couldn't keep their hands off each other"). Blue had surpassed Mitchell's status as a mere folk singer - both artistically and commercially - and she'd evolved from the musician at the end of the block to a major pop icon. Unlike other powerful female voices of the day, such as Tina Turner, Bonnie Raitt, and Joan Baez, whose power was associated with battle-ready sexual ferocity or political relevance, Joni's impact was simply musical. Her new compositions were well-crafted, and her voice, as well as her distinctive and wide-toned acoustic guitar playing, remained strong and rich even as it scaled octaves like a big bird swallowed by the sky. In contrast to Neil Young, whose art was heading in a much darker, self-destructive way, Joni's attendance at Mariposa represented positive musical and cultural transformation. If Canada was about to emerge from its patchouli fog of the 1960s, Joni was the hood ornament for a culture on the verge of a new era.

Joni must have appeared ethereal to Tex as she strolled along the canal banks: she had unblemished skin, high, sloping cheekbones, and a striking overbite.She was tall, as well, with praying mantis arms and the legs of a colt, favoring finely-fabricated Topanga Canyon dresses that swept the ground. Her presence was an early sign that, over the next few days, things on Centre Island would be very different than planned.

Leigh Cline served as the company's technical director. Even though we had a large crowd that weekend, there were no significant mistakes or incidents. I believe that someone touched me on the shoulder and said, 'They're here,' in retrospect. And it was our responsibility to handle all of that."

In 1972, organizers added a new element to the festival's layout: five or six tiny stages with simultaneous performances. "It was the first time anyone had tried it, but it's now the standard at most festivals," he said. "Because of this arrangement, we avoided booking large acts for whom the stages were too small. Activated Air, a Philadelphia-based sound company, brought in the system because nobody else in Canada had the necessary apparatus to accommodate so many stages. We downsized items on purpose to make them more manageable. Consequently," he added with a sneer, "this would be the year that the heavyweights decided to show up."

Ken Whiteley remarked, "Joni was simply Joni; she had been there previously. I saw her at the 1964 festival at Innes Lake, donning a long evening gown and golden hair. She was very distraught after her performance because a group of idiots had yelled at her while she was performing.
Organizers were initially concerned that Joni's appearance would be too much for the small festival to manage because, according to Cline, "the backstage area was only separated by a red snow fence, and we only had folkie security on site." However, there were no significant incidents. As the crowd and volunteers sailed across the harbor at dusk on Saturday, organizers gathered at the Executive Motor Hotel on the corner of King Street and Bathurst to wipe their brows, feeling relieved that they'd avoided any trouble.

Cline recalls returning to the Executive and thinking, "Well, we made it through. It's over. It wasn't a disaster." But then all of sudden the air escaped from the room. Someone walked in and said, "Well, guys, I just talked to [publicist] Richard Flohil. Bob Dylan's in town and he's coming to the island tomorrow."

No one can corroborate Dylan's presence on Saturday, despite the fact that Goddard quotes him as saying he was there. Bradley Hardy, age 15, is certain he saw him during Joni Mitchell's early evening mini-performance. He recalls seeing Dylan standing behind a snow fence while holding a white Styrofoam cup and conversing with people. We pulled out our cameras, and I'm fairly certain he was aware of our presence. I turned around and looked back at this juncture. This individual was approaching me along the same path. It was just me and Bob Dylan and it was incredible. I was immediately cognizant of the possibility. I was overcome, astonished, and full of adrenaline. I aimed and focused the camera at him, but he continued to approach. He needed only to pause for a moment, but he did not. As he passed by me and approached the stage, I snapped a few photographs. I have no idea what happened next. I don't believe he ever appeared on stage."

Michael Laderoute, a musician, concurs with Bradley that Dylan was present on Saturday. Someone told me that he was in attendance to see Leon Redbone, but I cannot confirm this. It would have made sense because they shared a musical affinity, at least Dylan did for Leon. Leon exuded an aura of mystique, and after Dylan's motorcycle accident, some individuals believed he was Bob in disguise. When Leon resided in Toronto, he was a figure of mystery. When asked how to contact him, he provided the number of a pool hall at the intersection of Yonge and Bloor. Someone would go get Grunt if you requested him by name. I quite admired him. He was an intriguing and talented musician.

Sunday morning, Dylan and Kathleen Miller, who was also a volunteer responsible for looking after Taj Mahal and his sibling, arrived on a boat. "Taj, his brother, and I boarded the small ferry with maybe twenty people seated near the front on the left," she explained. "Just as the ferry began to depart, this short man jumped on and began searching for a seat. I moved over. Taj approached him and inquired, 'Hey, buddy, how's it going? Are you going to play?' I noticed upon careful inspection that it was Dylan. The radio waves were filled with announcements that he was going to play earlier in the day, and as a consequence, the island was in complete chaos on Sunday. Certainly, I have told this story over the years. Bob Dylan plopped down beside me." Lightfoot arrived on the island around the same time as Dylan, but he concealed his presence. Lightfoot and Dylan eventually located one another on Sunday, but both were able to circulate for some time without being discovered.

After hearing the news for the first time, Cline sought confirmation. Richard Flohil stated that he had not actually seen Dylan, but had been informed that he would be present. Then, according to Cline, "after making a few phone calls, he returned and announced, 'We have a problem' " Cline stated, "Dylan was ten levels above Neil, Joni, and Gordon Lightfoot; he had an aura of mystery from the beginning." Consequently, festival administrators were faced with a unique situation: deciding whether or not the greatest songwriter of their generation should be permitted to affect the festival's health and stability as it unfolded that weekend on the small island at the bottom of the city.

The Dylanmania that ended up consuming the festival started as a slow boil. One of the people responsible for making sure that it did not affect the day's proceedings was area manager coordinator Marna Snitman, who, on Saturday, dropped Valium for the first (and last) time in order to smooth her fraying nerves. Because of the stars' presence, her fellow festival lieutenants met every five minutes to determine what to do with all of the surprise performers. "In past festivals, I could just put away my board member hat and concentrate on helping the area managers.

Cooney explained to Dylan that while Joni Mitchell's performance the day before had gone well, he was concerned that Dylan's performance would negatively impact the festival. After saying this, Dylan "kind of just stood there and said nothing." Cooney recalled, "There was a strange adolescent with him who did all the talking." The child continued saying "but, but, but..." to respond to Bob. It was extremely odd. I do not know who this child was." While most people remembered the majority of Dylan's entourage, including his son Jesse, wife Sarah, musician David Bromberg, and friend Adam Mitchell of The Paupers, nobody recalled Cooney's "weird kid." Knowing what we do about the extraordinary nature of the event and the events of that week, it is as if Cooney's "weird kid" was conjured from the day's circumstances, a character born from a Dylan song.

After Dylan's return, the festival's tone shifted, and it wasn't long before he had to be forcibly removed from the island. Michael Laderoute stated, "after people discovered that he was there, there was all kinds of commotion. People were rowing boats across from the mainland trying to get to Centre Island, and some people were swimming across, too. It was pretty insane. There was this red snow-fencing around the perimeter, and I remember people trying to get to Dylan, who was being taken backstage. Security was trying to hold them back, but the fence was bending. It held, but you wonder what would have happened if it had snapped."

Dylan was observed leaving a workshop, and the crowd quickly gathered around the renowned musician. He was pursued by fans who left their blankets and rucksacks behind, and because it was Sunday, weekend revelers who had drained their wineskins and emptied their pipes would have gained additional fortitude. Hundreds of scruffy folksingers attempting to capture their hero must have been quite a sight. Dylan and his family moved with a chevron of festival staff, who brought him a second time to the ferry that transported him to the mainland. Pete Otis, a musician and publisher, was among those who pursued him. He recalls: "It was as if Jesus Christ himself were among us, and this was our chance to get near. We were all ecstatic that he was among us. My acquaintance turned to me after he was out of sight and said , 'Man, I don't know why I'm running. But I have to keep running.' Then, he just disappeared. It was symbolic in a way, because at the end of that day, everything just seemed a little different." Pete and the rest of the throng may have been pursuing more than just a man wearing a red bandana and cotton shirt. Perhaps they were in pursuit of themselves, their vitality, and the last remnants of their vanishing times.

Tex McLeod departed just after Dylan left. His companions returned the boat to its Oakville marina, and he was dropped off on the 401 that evening while hitchhiking home. A gentleman picked him up. When he gazed through the window, he saw the legendary singer Stan Rogers. Stan drove him to 115 as they discussed how incredible it was to be a part of such an incredible festival. While driving, they listened to the radio, which described how the RCMP had apprehended three more Millhaven inmates, leaving only four on the loose. The majority of the others would be apprehended by the end of the summer, including Donald Oag, who was discovered a few miles from the prison after attempting to return there from Ottawa, indicating he wished to be allowed back inside. The only remaining fugitive was Streto Dzambas, who had eluded police for four months until early November, when the Ontario Provincial Police (OPP) received a report from INTERPOL that a man matching Dzambas' description had been apprehended in rural Yugoslavia for nearly murdering his father. Dzambas served the remainder of his sentence in a Balkan penitentiary. The individuals who had escaped on July's second Tuesday evening were now contained. The spirits were forced back into their cage.

LETTER IN WHICH I TALK ABOUT WHAT I'M NOT SUPPOSED TO TALK ABOUT

Songs. They kept coming for you, Gord. Great songs, too: "Steel Rail Blues," "Pride of Man," and two Hall of Famers: "The Way I Feel" and "Early Morning Rain." Perhaps it is an exaggeration to claim that the last two compositions were the saddest and most poignant of their time, but why the hell not? Babies have taken flight. There is a loss. The guitar-playing vagrant is unable to pursue his ex-lover as he sees her leave. You construct in the lyrics – and in your persona – a place where toughness and melancholy coexist, where the world's forces have weakened the strong man.

With your first and second albums (The Way I Feel, the title track re-recorded with an electric ensemble), you toured relentlessly. You were playing everywhere and making a fortune. In Canada and the United States, radio stations frequently played your song. You were an eight-year overnight triumph pursuing your lifelong passion. The city of Orillia designated August 5, 1967 as "Gordon Lightfoot Day." Then followed "The Canadian Railroad Trilogy."

Oh, man.

1966, 1967, and 1968 were all tremendous years. However, I would not be writing this book if these events were not overshadowed by something sinister. As the writer Tom Hopkins stated in a 1978 article, "To talk of Lightfoot, you must talk of tragedy." My friend put it another way: "What defines us as we age is how we deal with not being at thirty where we thought we'd be at eighteen." I would add a qualification: what defines some of us is how we cope with being exactly where we envisioned we'd be at age thirty. I suppose this is a convoluted way of saying that there were complications and sacrifices throughout all of this, including the Carnegie Hall performances, Johnny Carson appearances, and your triumphant return to Massey Hall, not to mention the Mariposa appearances that occurred after you and Whelan were initially rejected by festival organizers. Your marriage was the first item to be sacrificed, as it never aligned with your pursuit of creative fulfillment. Desires. Now that's a term.

Okay, Gord, the heaviness is coming. However, first, a tale. It was located on the Internet. It's a fairly amusing excerpt. I'm playing you with humor here, Gord, because what follows a few paragraphs down is not particularly humorous. Regardless, here it is:
"Interviewer: So what have you got next in the way of records? How many times have you been asked that question?
(Lightfoot turns slightly and farts loudly into the microphone)."

Okay, Gord: the heaviest shit. Who knows how many of the stories I've heard are accurate? I am certain that some of them are complete nonsense, while others are not. I know. Someone once told me that one of the reasons you didn't want to talk to me – or any other writer like me – was because we'd ask you about the drinking and the drugs and the married life and being with Cathy Evelyn. Still, I trust that what I'm about to say does not offend you, because all I'm doing is attempting to comprehend without degrading something that, in all honesty, I can relate to and respect to the highest degree.

Okay, the drinking. It occurs. I am familiar with this firsthand. The majority of artists are musicians. What other job brings a tray of cold beers to your dressing room, along with a bottle of whiskey, a snort of cocaine, or a joint if your manager has phoned ahead and asked politely in cellphone whispers? If the pretty girl remains for your set, buys your record, and tells you that she digs your music, you might even go home with her for more drinks, although this rarely occurs. Typically, she grabs you or you grab her, and before you know it, it's morning and the bass player is attempting to wake you up by pounding on your door. On the next bus ride to wherever, you sleep in the back seat or, if you're fortunate, the bunk bed or banquette while listening to the idle chatter of your bandmates, whose conversation, inevitably, is about you and how it's been four weeks since this behavior began, and should they be concerned? Typically, they conclude that they should not be concerned and continue onward. Must continue with the job. One must pay one's expenses. Moreover, if the accommodations are spacious and comfortable and the music is pleasant, they will overlook any difficulty. When someone has the fortitude to confront you, you threaten them by swinging at them and possibly landing a blow, but your band disregards this. Occasionally they swing back, but by then their fate has already been determined. Screw them. You will do whatever you darn well please, and some shit-ass jobbing drummer has no right to tell you otherwise.

An acquaintance of mine is also a musician. When we first met, we were children, and rock and roll was our favorite activity. More and more people began attending his performances as his music improved. To get him to quit, other bands would have to evict him from their rehearsal spaces. We were both composing hundreds of compositions and performing four-hour concerts. Because we were proficient with our instruments, we could express any musical notions that occurred to us. We were youthful and felt robust. Long hours and interminable bus journeys did not matter to us.

One night, after my friend had been particularly unpleasant, I helped him into his apartment. Before he left, I asked him, "I'm curious as to what your fourteen-year-old self would say to your twenty-three-year-old self?" "You think there's something wrong with me?" he asked, leaning back in the passenger seat. I responded, "No, no. There is nothing wrong with you," because there was nothing wrong with you, not yet. I believed that, like anyone else, he could cease drinking if I held up a mirror in front of him. I explained, "It's just that you've been drinking a lot lately." He glanced at me and waved his arm while saying, "Awww, pfft." "It's okay." Then he became somewhat melancholy. "You think I need help or something?" I told him, "I dunno, yes, maybe. But perhaps you should cease." He regarded me. He did not see through me. Then he remarked, "Well, thanks, eh?" I told him no issue. Then he stumbled into his apartment after leaving the car.

The moment seems so innocent when compared to the subsequent years: sleeping with women just so he could stay in their nice apartments; spending all of his money on alcohol; showing up later and later for his band's rehearsals; getting aggressive at times and generally despising people and the world; nearly burning to death in a couple of apartment fires; appearing with a bandaged this or broken that after drunken mishaps; and fostering a lifestyle that lacked any semblance of respectability. Even when he did work, the task was excellent and the times were extremely enjoyable. Then, however, both the work and the good times struck a wall. After his seventh or eighth beverage, he became a sour drunk. He would complain about an existence that was supposed to be liberated and beautiful, but had become something else. Eventually, I'd had enough. I was depressed and exhausted. My acquaintance was evicted, prompting me and a few others to decide to take action. We attempted a pseudo-intervention, but in retrospect, it was likely too little, too late.

We had no notion what we were doing; the intervention was unsuccessful. Still, there was a glimmer of optimism. After a fight erupted, my companion stormed out of the room. I pursued him, as I had done numerous times before. I discovered him hiding in the backyard between the trees, trembling and weeping. I comforted him and reassured him that everything would be alright. It was as if I were holding a young infant and attempting to talk him out of his despair. Then, as we separated, I said,"You need help. You've got to stop." That was the moment when he should have admitted that he understood I was correct and that he would return to the group and accept their offer to pay for a stay at a nearby drug and alcohol rehabilitation center. Instead, he repeated what he'd said to me years earlier: "You think I need assistance or something? You seriously doubt I can handle this on my own?" I told him he was unable to do so. He regained composure and rejoined the meeting.

While supine on a cot, he stated, "Okay." "Tell me all of the terrible things that I've done." We achieved success. It was fortunate that he learned about it from us. The next day, however, one of our group members showed him compassion. She informed him that he could stay with her instead of attending detox. She assured him that everything would be great and that she would take care of him. When we asked her what the hell she was doing, she told us that she didn't believe it was reasonable to compel him to do something he didn't want to do. A few days later, he sent us an email informing us that he was severing ties with us; he no longer desired to be friends with anyone who had attempted to influence him. My acquaintance is an adult, and I am uncertain of his future. You returned, Gord, without even attending A.A. or participating in a twelve-step program; you simply found a psychiatrist you liked and stopped drinking. However, I do not believe that everyone is capable of doing the same. I do not know where he is going, and I often worry that he is destined for a place I would never want him to go.

I just returned from the Vancouver Art Gallery, which is why I am considering this topic as I write to you. At an exhibition, Chinese artist Song Dong displayed a collection of his mother's accumulated objects. There are countless bottles, shopping bags, fabrics, soap sachets, and other items strewn across blankets in the gallery, which spans three rooms and encompasses miles of space. My acquaintance was a bit of a packrat as well. His apartment was filled with trash, and I still have boxes of his possessions, including cassette recordings and newspaper magazine clippings, in my cellar. In any other situation, his room would have resembled a magnificent shambles, but it became a symbol of defeat, with old Christmas ornaments dangling from a lifeless tree.

After entering a different section of the gallery, I discovered a sculpture by the Korean artist Khan Lee. It was also appealing to the eye: a spiraling stack of cassette tapes extending from the floor to the ceiling. Obviously, my friend kept cassettes, but so did I; boxes of them, documenting old recordings of band rehearsals, demos, radio programs on which we had appeared, and albums acquired at garage sales. I did not observe one of his cassettes leaning over the gallery until I reached the peak of the sculpture. I thought about both my companion and the music. I appreciate the chance to share this information with you, Gord. You do not know either myself or him. However, you are now aware of this tragic tale, and I hope it will prove useful as you continue reading.

Before beginning, I was once advised. The individual is both a journalist and a writer. His home is located on the west coast.
I came across a sculpture by the Korean artist Khan Lee at the entrance to the gallery. It was also aesthetically pleasing: a spiraling stack of cassette recordings extending from floor to ceiling. Obviously, my friend kept tapes, but so did I; boxes of them, documenting old recordings of band rehearsals, demos, radio programs on which we had appeared, and albums salvaged from garage sales. I did not notice one of his cassettes leaning out over the gallery until I followed the sculpture to its apex. I considered my companion and the music. I appreciate the opportunity to share this with you, Gord. You do not know either him or myself. However, you are now aware of this tragic tale, and I trust it will be of some assistance when you read what follows.
Before I begin, someone once advised me. The individual is both a writer and a journalist. His residence is on the west coast.
"I went to see Lightfoot play at the Place Des Arts in Montreal. I went there with a group of people who were part of a drug and addiction group, of which I was a member, trying to deal with a heroin problem. The show was great, and Lightfoot was great. He'd gotten off the drugs and the booze and looked really healthy. Somehow word reached Gord that we were there, and so he got a

message to us telling us to stay after the show. So once it ended, we sat in our seats for twenty minutes as people filed out of the hall, and then Gord came out. He sat with us and talked with us – these total strangers – about our recovery for a long time. He didn't have to do it. He was just being himself and trying to support us through these times. It was a remarkable thing and I'll never forget it. You expect a lot of things from your heroes, but this, I never expected."

So, Gord, I'm curious: did it all begin with Cathy? Or did it begin earlier? When reading Cathy's book, you get the impression that you're already well into drinking, sexing, and substance use. You have stated, "I had a happy childhood, but then depression set in, and I've been battling it ever since." In a moment of complete candor, you told the press, "It's one of the reasons why I drink," but in the same breath, you boasted, "I'm a good Canadian drinker," and that, at the time, you were consuming at least one bottle of alcohol per day. My friend was similarly inconsistent, oscillating between admissions of emotional despair and pride in his ability to maintain his habit and lifestyle. If you were also combating depression and addiction, I doubt that Cathy was an effective therapist. Instead, you discovered an abusive twin with occasional episodes of passion to maintain mutual interest.

Cathy had previously been with Richard Manuel and had given birth to Levon's daughter, Tracey Lee, whom she had also abandoned. She provided you with a form of physical poetry, in addition to narcotics and a place to hide. You could place your insecurities, anxieties, and growing sense of darkness and mortality in her care. She simultaneously normalized and propelled the rock and roll lifestyle into a rapid and delectable orbit. She would allow you to do whatever you wished. She was a dark apparition who comforted you because she knew how messed up and difficult your life was. She understood that you believed you were a fraud – that every successful artist feels like a fraud, living the kind of life that most people can only dream of – and that you feared that your success would soon be devoured, and that God would one day steal from you the good fortune and luck that had sustained your career while others were back home selling insurance or performing cover songs.

You had to suppress these concerns at home. We all did. We did not want to bring our crap into the lives of our loved ones. This is why gigging was so essential, and why gatherings were as well. Despite the fact that Cathy writes about how messed up things were, she also discusses the concerts and how you could do whatever you wanted with your music. You had complete control over your compositions, despite the fact that your life was spiraling out of control at the time.

Everyone discusses the theatrical performances. They describe how you used to sweep your hand over the body of your instrument and how the notes would descend like the feathers of a soft-shedding beast, with chords like butterscotch and your voice like hard candy. Once upon a time, it was acceptable to appear calm and composed on stage, with one finger on the mercury catch of a long glass thermometer to regulate the room's temperature. It wasn't about instant detonation: a cheap clowning blast of incendiary surprise that leaves nothing but stale smoke in the room. Back then, in the halls and velvet theaters, you would slipper to your spot beside a stool that held a water jug and a few sheets of lyrics, pausing to draw in the expectations and uncertainties of the audience, utter a few disarming words, and, slowly, carefully, demonstrate your quiet power, and whatever might explode would explode from within: an emotional rupture, a fissure of release in the darkened chamber that held what needed to be released. Some nights, no rainfall was recorded. On occasion, the brutes sat there unable to move, but thank God you were traveling. Thank God you weren't so obstinate as to bleed more than necessary for the ungrateful saps in Canton, Ohio, Madison, Wisconsin, or Albany, New York, who sat expressionless in establishments named The Smiling Parrot, Uncle Jo

After performances, there were innumerable hotel rooms. When we traveled, we always stayed at the dreadful Sandman Inn, whereas you presumably stayed in better accommodations. Still, you'd go to your hotel room: brown drapes, an airbrushed painting of a town other than the one you were in affixed to the headboard, two water glasses on the wooden nightstand, and the crumbs of the previous night's traveling shower-ring salesman seeding the edges of the wall where he'd eaten crackers while masturbating to Barbi Benton being interviewed by Mike Douglas on a shaky TV that trembled when you thumbed the.

Sometimes, you had a friend, even though you had Cathy, and, for a time, Brit, waiting at home. During the show, she'd been sitting close to the stage fucking you with her eyes while you played or sometimes she appeared out of the club's shadows, a brunette with a leather shoulder bag. Sometimes she followed you back to your room because someone else she'd been with had stayed in the same hotel the week before and sometimes you cared that she'd been with him but most times you did not, because if it was purity you were looking for you were in the wrong game. Sometimes she was charcoal-drawn wearing mostly black with boots up to her asscheeks and sometimes she was the mayor's daughter straight out of high school wanting to drink from the poisoned well of adulthood. Sometimes they came because they were curious about how you put together your songs and sometimes they wanted your dick as a trophy and sometimes they thought they could show you something that was wilder than what you'd seen on tour, which, if you'd just swung through the American midwest or Thunder Bay, it probably was not. Sometimes they'd want to hold your hand for a while or talk about books or discuss politics, and sometimes they couldn't wait to crack open the booze and tear off their clothes and hit the bed or carpet busy and fast. Sometimes they'd say "Nice room," or "Hey, can I see your guitar?" or "Do you want to have a shower?" or, in your case, maybe they said, "You know, I orgasmed the first time I heard 'If You Could Read My Mind.' " Sometimes, they'd want to talk before sex, and sometimes they'd want to talk after. Sometimes they wanted the lights on and sometimes they wanted them off and sometimes they brought their own things, like ropes or handcuffs or vibrators or Polaroid cameras or creams or oils or, once, a purse with these little cables and an electric box which you plugged in before fastening them to her nipples, which is actually something that happened to another musician I know. Sometimes they cried afterwards and sobbed, "How could I do this to him?" and sometimes they wanted to stay and sometimes they asked for your shirt as a souvenir and sometimes they told you about what the bass player from a lesser band was like and sometimes they wanted you to meet their parents and sometimes they just got dressed and got the fuck out, which, sometimes, you preferred.

Gale Zoe Garnett told me about sleeping with you. In San Francisco, after her band, Gale Garnett and the Gentle Reign, opened for you. I didn't go around looking for people you'd slept with, Gord. I don't care, not really. Gale is a very open and honest person, and when we were talking, she just said it. She told me, "The following morning I gave him a necklace of olive green Peking beads. He told me, 'I've been here (in San Francisco) for a few days, and no one has given me beads.' He seemed kind of hurt by it, so I gave him mine. Gord was a very straight Scottish Presbyterian guy. He wasn't putting me on. He was very touched by it. He was, in a way, a terrific innocent. I think that he was always looking for Laura Secord in the middle of a dirty movie, searching for that purity somehow. Bobby Neuwirth, Dylan's friend, had been with us earlier and he was a very toxic presence. He said, 'You just want to blow him.' I told him, 'No way! I'm not even good at that.' To be honest, everyone was drunk, and I didn't think that it was the best thing for Gord to climb into a vehicle at that point. It was very sweet, very innocent. It was the sixties, sure, but it didn't feel like it that night, not once we were alone."

Another woman told me stuff, then another, then another. They weren't hard to find, Gord. Some were less forgiving than others. One of them told me that you gave her what you considered to be the highest compliment possible. You compared her to "my true love, Cathy." Another said that you wanted "something wild one last time." Finally, another told me: "I loved the artist and liked the sad man. Though he was just a man, I wouldn't have done it."

Drugs and alcohol go hand-in-hand with intercourse in the same way that rain follows a thick bank of storm clouds. The years 1970 through 1972 were terrible. In her chapter titled "That's What You Get for Loving Me," Cathy claims you were high on pills when you suspended her upside down from a twenty-story balcony in Hawaii. A security guard began banging on the door, and he convinced you not to abandon her. Cathy claims that you once shoved her head into the commode. You responded to this allegation by saying, "It was a clean toilet bowl," to Maynard Collins. If there was something in it, I would not have done that under any circumstances." Cathy claims that you also struck her, fracturing her cheekbone with a single blow. She required cosmetic surgery, which you covered. Cathy fought back, of course, and the situation quickly degenerated into a terrible shitstorm of pain and animosity. It was The Days of Wine and Roses all over again: two individuals who had become cruel to themselves, each other, and themselves. Despite this, Cathy rebounded rubbery and unfettered, even after the worst of times. Then you would return to your band to continue creating the greatest collection of Canadian compositions ever. What the hell?! Excuse the fans, or at least some of us, for imagining you as a heroic party monster with the ability to write amazing songs while completely out of your mind.

I have attempted to locate Cathy Evelyn Smith, but I am unfamiliar with her. A few years ago, she was arrested in Vancouver's East Side for possession of contraband, and nobody has heard from her since.

THE END OF THE WEEKEND

Bob Dylan's departure from Mariposa '72 was immediately followed by Neil Young's appearance. True to form, he passed through the scene like a ghost, arriving on the island unnoticed. During the height of Dylanmania, his presence was not as strongly felt, nor was it as significant an organizational burden. Neil spent most of his time alone in the tent with his new wife Carrie Snodgrass. Snodgress was six months pregnant when she gave birth to Neil's first son, Zeke, in September. Bruce Cockburn wound up sharing his set time with Young, which made him "slightly resentful," as he put it. The twenty-six-year-old songwriter played four tracks on acoustic guitar: "Helpless," "Heart of Gold," "Sugar Mountain," and "Harvest." He had just completed a tour in support of his number one album, Harvest. Although it is unclear why he visited Mariposa, he was not unrelated to the festival.

 In actuality, Neil's performance at Mariposa would be one of the last instances of unadulterated balladry before the songwriter pushed his repertoire headfirst into the ditch, disregarding the demands of conventional hit-making. His music became more poignant as the decade veered toward North American economic decline, pornography, hostage danger, fast food, squalor, and dangerous drugs. Neil Young's Mariposa '72 was the last time he allowed his art to bask in providence under the warmth of the sun. It was a subtle gift to the fans, their city, and their scene, one last gesture before gutting his sound from the inside out and gaining a head start on the forces that would make peace and love their girlfriend.

On Sunday, just as you, Bob, Neil, and Joni were coming together, the Pioneer 10 spacecraft passed through the asteroid belt without incident. I don't want to come across as a hippy, Gord, but I believe that things like the penetration of the solar system are essential to the earth, which is an integral part of that system and all. The event occurred far away, but people must have perceived it: a wave that rippled across the sky imperceptibly. In addition, it occurred almost a week to the day after the total solar eclipse that Carly Simon wrote about in her song "You're So Vain." I wonder whether what was happening in the sky made you sit down by yourself to play even though there was no stage, no mics, or no lighting, because, from what people tell me, you are very particular about that sort of thing.

Finally, you have returned, and you have returned strong. You consistently had hit records, Gord. "Sundown" was about to enter the world. So too was "The Wreck of the Edmund Fitzgerald," and did I mention that? Just as I was completing this book, I performed that song at the Horseshoe as part of this seventies Juno night, with our old bass player Tim singing the song for the first time in at least a decade.

We were the support act for Tragically Hip. I know you are familiar with them because in 2009 you performed a concert with Gord Downie, which was more of an interview-concert. I heard it was wonderful, but I couldn't attend. Anyway, after soundcheck ended that afternoon in Detroit, Tim, the song's singer, went for a walk to locate the Maritime Sailors Museum, which you sing about in the song. Due to the fact that we were the opening act, we had not intended to perform the song. On that tour, we had limited stage time, so we packed our set with shorter tracks. When Tim returned, he asked if I thought we should play it, to which I replied, "Absolutely," despite the fact that it would take up approximately a quarter of our set. So we did. That was our final song. When it concluded, the audience stood and applauded. It would be the only occurrence of its kind throughout the tour, and the only time we would perform the song.

Dan Hill additionally played at the Horseshoe. We performed "Sometimes When We Touch" with him, which concluded the evening. It was remarkable. Everyone was singing and going insane, and you could literally feel the floor lifting off the ground. Dan told me a tale about you and Tim Hardin a few days later. It also pertains to you and Dan. It proceeds as follows:

"Gord was good to a lot of musicians. Tim Hardin stayed with him just before he died, and he was going through terrible methadone withdrawal. Gord was quite concerned and so, one time, when it was particularly bad, Gord asked, 'Can I go out and get you some aspirin or something?' Hardin looked at him like he was crazy. But Gord was just trying to help.

"I never saw the mean or angry side of Gord, even though, you know, I'd heard stories. He was always sweet to me. In 1977, I was having really bad girlfriend problems. She told me that she never wanted to see me again and she kicked me out. I'd been in love with her since I was fifteen years old. I'd finished a show in Moncton and I figured that the only chance I had to reconcile with her was going to happen that night if it happened at all, but I had a show in St. John, N.B., the following day. Bernie Fiedler said 'Let's call Lightfoot and see if we can borrow his Lear Jet.' Gord told me, 'Ya, I can get you this jet on five thousand dollars credit, and I'll front you the money.' It was such a generous thing to do. After I thanked him, he said, 'But I'll tell you right now, there ain't no woman in the world who's worth five thousand dollars.' It was such a perfect Lightfoot quote. I'll never forget this Learjet coming into Moncton airport at two in the morning. Gord had just come through his huge divorce, so he might have been extra sympathetic, I don't know." In his book, Collins wrote that when Brita's lawyer left the courtroom, he was humming one of your songs, "That's What You Get For Lovin' Me."

At the Horseshoe, Dan Hill also played. We did "Sometimes When We Touch" with him, and it ended the night. It was spectacular. Everyone was singing along and going crazy and you could feel the floor being lifted off the ground. A few days later, Dan told me a story about you and Tim Hardin. It's also about you and Dan. It goes like this:
"Gord was good to a lot of musicians. Tim Hardin stayed with him just before he died, and he was going through terrible methadone withdrawal. Gord was quite concerned and so, one time, when it was particularly bad, Gord asked, 'Can I go out and get you some aspirin or something?' Hardin looked at him like he was crazy. But Gord was just trying to help.
"I never saw the mean or angry side of Gord, even though, you know, I'd heard stories. He was always sweet to me. In 1977, I was having really bad girlfriend problems. She told me that she never wanted to see me again and she kicked me out. I'd been in love

with her since I was fifteen years old. I'd finished a show in Moncton and I figured that the only chance I had to reconcile with her was going to happen that night if it happened at all, but I had a show in St. John, N.B., the following day. Bernie Fiedler said 'Let's call Lightfoot and see if we can borrow his Lear Jet.' Gord told me, 'Ya, I can get you this jet on five thousand dollars credit, and I'll front you the money.' It was such a generous thing to do. After I thanked him, he said, 'But I'll tell you right now, there ain't no woman in the world who's worth five thousand dollars.' It was such a perfect Lightfoot quote. I'll never forget this Learjet coming into Moncton airport at two in the morning. Gord had just come through his huge divorce, so he might have been extra sympathetic, I don't know." In his book, Collins wrote that when Brita's lawyer left the courtroom, he was humming one of your songs, "That's What You Get For Lovin' Me."

Regardless, he emailed me to inform me that you had passed away, or at the very least, that there were allegations throughout his Globe and Mail newsroom that you had passed away. A stomach aneurysm that resulted in a stroke had just occurred, so the news did not come as a surprise, though it was undoubtedly sorrowful and upsetting. You were at home when you passed away. Only you weren't dead. Not yet. But I need not tell you that.

Here is what I believe; Gord, try not to get angry. I believe you are acting. You or a known individual. I believe you were watching the Opening Ceremonies with these other musicians, k.d. Lang and Neil Young, getting a chance to perform, and in a moment of mischief, you thought you would attempt to bring the nation's thoughts back to the source: back to you. It's a ridiculous hypothesis, I agree. Probably, it is absurd. But I believe that to be the case. During that event, the nation may have needed to recall the factors that contributed to this level of national pride and enthusiasm.

In this book, I didn't want to get anybody in trouble, especially not you, Gord. And I don't want to get th
e person who gave me the information in trouble, either.

Previously, your grandeur was either defined by your music or by your persona, which, for some, negated your greatness. Now, however, the situation is nearly reversed. You haven't had a hit record in decades, but you still play "Black Day in July" at charity auctions in small towns and call superfans like Char Westbrook – who writes about you, posts pictures of you on the Internet, and operates websites and forums dedicated to you – to wish them a happy birthday. Once, Sylvia Tyson told me: "Gordon is much more open than before. Much more gregarious. He used to be very self-contained, very driven. But now it seems as if he's finally enjoying the fruits of his labors. There was a time when all he wanted was to be in the mainstream of pop music, but that's not an issue anymore. I'm glad that I know Gordon at this stage in his life. A lot of people are."

Thus, the scumbag is resurrected. An excellent phoenix. Not only are you evidently no longer a scumbag, but you also provided the author who wrote about you with a conclusion for his book.

I feel fine after writing this. I wonder how you feel. There is an exhilaration that comes with finishing a book, and you may be experiencing a similar exhilaration as you near the conclusion of your career, legacy, and life. Perhaps you, too, are elated – or perhaps you're relieved – because there are likely many other topics I could have included in this book but did not.

Sorry. Being so near to the end, this type of nonsense can sometimes just flow out. It is my final opportunity to express what I feel inside. After what transpired at Mariposa on Sunday, when four of the world's finest songwriters gathered on a small island at the bottom of my city – your city, our city – you continued drinking and doing the other things you did. There were ups and downs, but you eventually emerged victorious. In that instant on the island, everything was straightforward. You retrieved your guitar from its case and borrowed a pick from someone else. There was Cathy Evelyn standing behind you. Under the trees, it was shady and cool, and people began to congregate quietly, as opposed to their maniacal pursuit of Dylan. You sipped a beer while surveying the entire field. You ejaculated and placed your hand on the fretboard. You were at home, where the grass was velvety.

Manufactured by Amazon.ca
Acheson, AB

12061608R00063